WHAT'S
—in the—
BIBLE?

A CONCISE LOOK AT THE 39 BOOKS OF THE HEBREW BIBLE

Lillian C. Freudmann

JASON ARONSON INC.
Northvale, New Jersey
London

The author gratefully acknowledges permission to reproduce the following material:

Maps on pages 50 and 103 copyright © Carta Ltd. Used by permission.

Map on page 20 used by permission of *Biblical Archaeology Review*.

Maps on pages 26 and 30 are from THE WESTMINSTER HISTORICAL ATLAS TO THE BIBLE by George Ernest Wright and Floyd Vivian Filson. Used by permission of Westminster John Knox Press.

This book was set in 12 pt. Garamond by Alpha Graphics of Pittsfield, New Hampshire.

Copyright © 1996 by Lillian C. Freudmann

10 9 8 7 6 5 4 3 2 1

Library of Congress Cataloging-in-Publication Data
Freudmann, Lillian C.
    What's in the Bible? : a concise look at the 39 books of the
    Hebrew Bible / Lillian C. Freudmann.
        p.   cm.
    Includes bibliographical references (p.   ) and index.
    ISBN 1-56821-602-5 (alk. paper)
    1. Bible.   O.T.—Outlines, syllabi, etc.   I. Title.
BS1193.F74   1996
221.6'1—dc20   96-4776
                                                 CIP

Manufactured in the United States of America. Jason Aronson Inc. offers books and cassettes. For information and catalog write to Jason Aronson Inc., 230 Livingston Street, Northvale, New Jersey 07647.

To Varda, Carol, and George,
With love and appreciation

CONTENTS

MAPS

INTRODUCTION

This book is an outgrowth of my experience teaching the Bible to children and adults. It is also a consequence of the reactions I encountered from numerous people when they learned of my vocation.

I often found people defensive and apologetic for their unfamiliarity with the Bible. They invariably had tried to read it and got discouraged with the genealogies in the early part of the first book. Finding this boring and expecting more of the same in subsequent books, they gave up in despair.

Since the Bible is a collection of many books on different subjects—of events in the hoary past, in far-off lands where customs, language, and life-styles differ radically from our own—it is often challenging, if not intimidating, to penetrate that world of literature. Whether they are students in a classroom or casual, curious readers, people usually want to know "what the book is about" before starting to read it. Once they have an idea about the contents, they often feel more comfortable about delving into it.

In this volume I have attempted to summarize the contents of the thirty-nine books of the Hebrew Bible. In this way, potential readers of the Bible can get an idea of the plot or storyline in each book.

To make the events related in the Bible more under-standable, I have put them in a historical context by providing a time line of biblical and Jewish history and a chronological table of the kings of Israel and Judah, as well as brief explanations of the prevailing social, economic, and religious conditions that provoked or motivated the writers of many books. I have also en-deavored to explain the reasons for the inclusion of certain books in the canon that, on the surface, may seem unlikely candidates for a collection of holy books. There are maps to help locate places mentioned in the Bible and to illustrate some of the events, such as the exodus from Egypt, the settlement of the twelve tribes in Israel, and the route of the exiles to and from Babylon.

The Bible is replete with beautiful phrases, many of which people use today and of whose origin they may not be aware. I have included with the summary of each book some of the famous and eloquent verses found therein. Often a particular verse expresses succinctly the essence of the book or its author. Although I availed myself of standard Bible translations, I used my own words in those verses where I thought my translation was clearer and closer to the meaning of the original Hebrew.

This work is not meant as a substitute for reading the Bible any more than Charles and Mary Lamb's summa-ries of Shakespeare's plays are meant to replace the Bard. Rather, I hope that this little volume will encourage the reading and study of the Book of Books.

NAMES AND CONTENTS OF THE HEBREW AND CHRISTIAN BIBLES

The Jewish or Hebrew Bible = (Old Testament) = *Tanakh*
The Protestant Bible = Hebrew Bible + New Testament
Eastern Orthodox and Roman Catholic Bible = Hebrew
 Bible + Apocrypha + New Testament

The Hebrew Bible consists of thirty-nine books divided into three main sections:

NAME IN HEBREW	ENGLISH	GREEK
Torah	Five Books of Moses	Pentateuch
Nevi'im	Prophets	Prophetai
Ketuvim	Holy Writings	Hagiographa

TORAH, OR FIVE BOOKS OF MOSES

Genesis
Exodus
Leviticus
Numbers
Deuteronomy
 Total: five books

NEVI'IM, OR PROPHETS

Early Prophets

  Joshua
  Judges
  1, 2 Samuel
  1, 2 Kings

Later Prophets

  Isaiah
  Jeremiah
  Ezekiel

Twelve "Minor" Prophets

  Hosea
  Joel
  Amos
  Obadiah
  Jonah
  Micah
  Nahum
  Habakkuk
  Zephaniah
  Haggai
  Zechariah
  Malachi

Total: twenty-one books

KETUVIM, OR HOLY WRITINGS

the five Scrolls or Megillot

Psalms	Song of Songs	Daniel
Proverbs	Ruth	Ezra
Job	Lamentations	Nehemiah
	Ecclesiastes	1, 2 Chronicles
	Esther	

Total: thirteen books

HISTORICAL PERIODS AND DATES OF CANONIZATION IN THE HEBREW BIBLE BOOKS

The books in the Hebrew Bible cover a long period of history, beginning with its concept of Creation and continuing to Noah. The dating of these events is speculative and dependent on an individual's religious beliefs. In more historical times, the narratives in the Hebrew Bible extend from Abraham, in about 2000 B.C.E., to Ezra, in the fourth century B.C.E.

As shown earlier in this chapter, the Hebrew Bible, or *Tanakh*, is divided into three main sections. The division represents three distinct stages in the process of canonization of the Bible books. The finalizing of the first part of the Bible, the Torah (or Pentateuch), occurred during the Babylonian Exile, probably in the sixth century B.C.E. The Prophetic section of the Bible was canonized during the Persian period, about the fourth century B.C.E. The Holy Writings, which constitute the third section of the Bible, were canonized over a period extending from about the second century B.C.E. to the second century C.E.

The divisions into which the Jews arranged their Bible are based, not only on *time of canonization*, but also on *degrees of sacredness*. The holiest books make up the Pentateuch, next are those in the Prophetic section, and the last are the books in the Hagiographa. It was believed that the Torah contained the words of God, the Prophetic books reported His messages to the Prophets, and the authors of the Hagiographa were men inspired by God.

The books of the Apocrypha and Pseudepigrapha overlapped the period when the third division of the Hebrew Bible was being canonized and most of the New Testament books were being composed.

It should be noted that only eleven of the fourteen books of the Apocrypha were canonized by the Roman Catholic, Greek Orthodox, and Byzantine Orthodox Churches. The Russian and Syrian Orthodox Churches did not canonize any of the books of the Apocrypha.

Important Dates
in Jewish History

BEFORE THE COMMON ERA (B.C.E.)[1]

2000–1850	Age of the Patriarchs: Abraham, Isaac, Jacob, and Jacob's twelve sons
1850–1440	Israelites in Egypt (see Exodus 12:40–41)
1440	Exodus from Egypt
1440–1400	Wandering in the wilderness
1400	Beginning of the conquest of the Promised Land
1400–1030	Period of the Judges (see 1 Kings 6:1)
1060–1010	Age of Samuel: priest, prophet, judge, and kingmaker
1030	Establishment of the Kingdom of Israel
1030–932	The United Kingdom: Judah and Israel
1030–1006	Reign of King Saul
1011–971	Reign of King David
971–932	Reign of King Solomon
932	Divided Kingdoms of Judah and Israel

---

1. All dates are approximate and follow biblical chronology, where applicable. This chronology does not include Jewish history in the Diaspora. It focuses instead on historical movements as they affected the people and land of Israel (or Judah/Judea) in the Middle East.

932–721	Kingdom of Israel
721	Fall of Israel to Assyria; exile and dispersion of the Ten Tribes of Israel
932–586	Kingdom of Judah[2]
597	First exile: of the king, aristocracy, and artisans to Babylonia. Daniel, as a member of the aristocracy, is one of the exiles
586	Fall of Judah; destruction of the Temple in Jerusalem; exile of most Judeans to Babylonia
538	Defeat of Babylonia by Persia and conquest of its empire by Cyrus; Judah falls under Persian rule
538–332	Persian Period; Cyrus's decree that Jews could return to Jerusalem with Temple vessels taken by the Babylonians and could rebuild the Temple
537	Zerubabel, a civil and political leader, and Jeshua, a religious leader, lead the first return to Jerusalem
536–534	Altar and foundation of the Temple built
529–520	Sabotage and slander by the Samaritans cause cessation of work on the Temple
520	Decree of Darius the Great permitting the resumption of work on the Temple
520–516	Prophets Haggai and Zechariah inspire Jews to resume work on the Temple
516	Completion and dedication of the Second Temple exactly seventy years after the destruction, as predicted by Jeremiah
485–465	Reign of Xerxes I (Ahasueros)

---

2. Actually, the Judean kingdom lasted 444 years, 1030–586 B.C.E.

482	Marriage of Esther
465–424	Reign of Artaxerxes I
460–445	Prophet Malachi in Jerusalem; finds demoralized conditions
444	Nehemiah's first visit to Jerusalem; strengthens its security and religious solidarity
432	Nehemiah's second visit to Jerusalem; halts desecration of the Temple and makes social and religious reforms
404–358	Reign of Artaxerxes II
397–380	Ezra in Jerusalem; develops the Great Synagogue (*HaKnesset HaGedola*) into an institution for Jewish teaching; makes lasting religious reforms and abolishes intermarriages
332	Defeat of Persian Empire by Alexander the Great; Judea under Hellenistic rule
323	Death of Alexander and division of his empire; Babylonia and Syria under the Seleucids and Egypt under the Ptolemies
332–165	Hellenistic Period
310–198	Judea under the Ptolemies of Egypt
245	Septuagint, Greek translation of the Torah, by Jews in Alexandria, Egypt
198–168	Judea under Seleucids of Syria
168	Antiochus IV ascends the throne, desecrates the Temple and promulgates anti-Jewish laws; start of the Maccabean revolt
168–134	Maccabean wars
165	The Temple is liberated and rededicated (Hanukah)
165–63	Hasmonean rule in Judea: Judah, 165–160; Jonathan, 160–143; Simon, 143–135; John Hyrcanus, 135–104; Judah Aristobulus, 104–

103; Alexander Yannai, 103–76, and his wife Salome Alexandra, 76–67; Aristobulus II, 67–63

63   Independence of Judea is lost with the rivalry between the brothers Aristobulus II and Hyrcanus II, who both appeal to Rome. Rome moves into the breach; Pompey brings Judea under Roman rule after conquering Jerusalem and Judea becomes a Roman province

47   Antipater, an Idumean (Edomite), appointed procurator of Judea

37–4   Herod, Antipater's son, becomes governor of Galilee and then king of Judea. Hasmonean dynasty is terminated by Herod's murder of all surviving descendants, including Herod's wife and sons. Herod declares himself king of Judea

37 B.C.E.– Herodian Period
70 C.E.

COMMON ERA (C.E.)

6   Rome assumes direct rule in Judea
26–36   Pontius Pilate becomes governor of Judea
67–73   First Jewish War against Rome. Destruction of the Temple; exile of the Jews. Fall of Masada; rise of Christianity
73   Shift from a sacrificial Temple cult to synagogue prayer service with an emphasis on good deeds
70–324   Roman Period; spread of Christianity with attendant antisemitism

73–425	Importance of the Sanhedrin as the supreme political, religious, and judicial body for Jews in Israel and the Diaspora
132–135	Second Jewish War against Rome led by Bar Kokhba; martyrdom of Rabbi Akiba
200–225	Redaction of the Mishnah by Judah haNasi
306–337	Constantine makes Christianity the state religion
324–640	Byzantine Period
400	Redaction of the Jerusalem Talmud
425	Sanhedrin is disbanded by the Roman government under pressure of the Christian Church
ca. 500	Redaction of the Babylonian Talmud
624	Rise of Islam with Mohammed's introduction of the new religion
640–1099	Arab Period; spread of Islam to dominant position in Middle East; forced conversion of entire populations
1096–1291	Crusader Period
1100–1500	Blood libels, massacres, plunder, forced conversions, and expulsions of Jews from England, France, Germany, and Spain. In many cases Jews had lived in these countries for 500 years, longer than the Christian population.
1291–1516	Mameluke Period: military caste of former slaves who ruled from Turkey to Egypt
1517–1914	Turkish Period: Turkish domination of all Middle Eastern countries including Palestine (Israel)

1914–1948 Britain and France divide the Middle East
           between themselves after World War I.
           Eventually, both have to leave their colo-
           nies. Israel is among the last liberated
1948   Establishment of the State of Israel

1

THE TORAH
(OR PENTATEUCH OR
FIVE BOOKS OF MOSES)

The books in the Torah contain narratives of the early history of the Hebrew people (later called Jews) and the laws that were given them to guide them throughout their existence. Historical events and legal material are interspersed. There are no separate categories of history, religion, law, and medicine in the Pentateuch. They are all aspects of Judaism as reflected in the Bible.

GENESIS

The first book of the Bible literally starts "in the beginning," with the creation of the world and all that is in it: light, sky, seas and land, heavenly bodies, fish and birds, animals and man (Adam).

The stories following creation deal with mankind's relation to this new world:

The Garden of Eden and its idyllic life was terminated when Adam and Eve disobeyed God and yielded to temptation.

Adam and Eve's sons, Cain and Abel, depict fratricidal rivalry that ended with the murder of Abel and the punishment of Cain to wander the earth.

Another son, Seth, was born to Adam and Eve.

Cain and Seth's descendants multiplied on the earth.

A growing corruption in mankind culminated in a deluge.

Noah and the Flood:

Noah built an ark, according to God's instructions, in which to house his family and animals during the coming flood.

Noah's sons, Shem, Ham, and Japheth, became the ancestors of many nations.

God's Covenant with Noah proclaimed seven ethical laws incumbent on all mankind to obey.

About 2000 B.C.E.

The Story of Abraham: the first Hebrew and the first monotheist: He obeyed God's command to leave his homeland in Mesopotamia and to migrate to Canaan, the land God promised to him and his descendants. He went with his wife, Sarah, and his nephew, Lot.

Sodom and Gemorrah were destroyed because of their wickedness. Only Lot and his two daughters survived. Each daughter seduced her father while he was drunk. Their sons were the ancestors of Moab and Ammon.

Sarah was barren for decades and therefore gave her handmaid, Hagar, to Abraham. She bore Ishmael.

God's Covenant with Abraham: Abraham and all the males in his household, as well as all his male descendants, were to be circumcised as an outward sign of this Covenant. God promised a son to Abraham and Sarah who would perpetuate Abraham's line and continue the Covenant. Ishmael would beget many descendants but was not part of the spiritual heritage of Abraham's descendants.

The Birth of Isaac: Ishmael and Hagar were sent away to assure Isaac's heritage.

The Binding of Isaac and the lessons derived from it: Abraham's faith was confirmed. God does not want human sacrifice.

Eliezer, Abraham's steward, was sent to find a wife for Isaac among his master's kin. He brought back Rebecca.

Sarah's death and burial in the Cave of the Machpelah: It became the family burial ground. Abraham purchased it, at a very high price, from Ephron the Hittite.

Abraham took another wife, Keturah, with whom he had six sons. They were sent away with gifts so as not to compete with Isaac and his special role as his father's heir.

Abraham died and was buried in the Cave of the Machpelah, where all the patriarchs and matriarchs except Rachel are buried.

Isaac and Rebecca were the parents of twins, Esau and Jacob. Esau was a hunter, favored by his father. Jacob, a sensitive and wiser son, was favored by his mother and was destined to be the next patriarch. Esau sold his birthright for a mess of pottage (stew). Jacob "stole" the blessing meant for the firstborn. Jacob then fled from his brother and left Canaan.

Jacob and his Family

Jacob's dream of a ladder ascending to heaven: God repeated the promise He had made to Abraham that the land was destined for Jacob's descendants.

Jacob came to his uncle, Laban, in Haran, where he lived for twenty years.

Jacob loved Rachel but was tricked into marrying Leah, her sister. He then also married Rachel. Eventually, he also acquired their handmaids, Bilha (of Rachel) and Zilpa (of Leah).

Jacob and Leah and Rachel

LEAH'S CHILDREN	BILHA'S SONS	ZILPA'S SONS	RACHEL'S SONS
1. Reuben	5. Dan	7. Gad	11. Joseph
2. Simeon	6. Naphtali	8. Asher	12. Benjamin
3. Levi			
4. Judah			
9. Issachar			
10. Zebulun			
Deena			

After twenty years Jacob returned to Canaan with his wives, children, and possessions.

Jacob wrestled with an angel of God, and his name was changed to Israel. His descendants were called the children of Israel, or Israelites.

Jacob and Esau met and parted peacefully.

The Episode of Deena and Shechem

Shechem, a Canaanite, seduced Deena and wanted to marry her. The men of his tribe underwent circumcision in order to intermarry with Jacob's descendants. Simeon and Levi acted treacherously, killing the men while they were recuperating from circumcision. Jacob severely condemned their actions.

Rachel died in childbirth with Benjamin at Efrat, near Bethlehem, where she is buried.

The Story of Joseph

Joseph was the favored son of Jacob. He was envied by his brothers because of their father's favoritism and resented for his arrogant behavior.

The brothers plotted to dispose of Joseph, who was subsequently sold into Egypt by Ishmaelites (*not* his brothers). His brothers told Jacob that Joseph had been killed by a wild animal.

Joseph was sold to Potiphar, to whom he became a loyal servant. He was falsely accused and imprisoned. He interpreted dreams while in prison.

He was called by the Pharaoh to interpret his dreams.

Joseph was appointed governor of Egypt, second to Pharaoh. He organized the collecting and storing of grain in anticipation of the famine he predicted. He was in charge of the distribution and sale of grain.

The famine in Canaan brought Joseph's brothers to Egypt to buy grain. Joseph recognized them.

The family was united as Jacob and his eleven sons and their families came to Egypt and were settled in Goshen, northeast Egypt, near Sinai.

Jacob blessed his sons and grandsons before his death. His sons buried him in the Cave of the Machpelah.

The Israelites remained in Egypt for 400 years, in the course of which they were enslaved.

Famous Verses in Genesis

1:1	In the beginning God created the heaven and the earth.
2:3	God blessed the seventh day and hallowed it because on it He rested from all His work. . . .
4:9	. . . am I my brother's keeper?
9:1	God blessed Noah and his sons and said to them, "Be fruitful and multiply and replenish the earth."
12:1	The Lord said to Abraham, "Leave your country, your homeland, and your father's house for the land I will show you."
12:3	I will bless those who bless you and he who curses you, I will curse.
21:12	God said to Abraham: ". . . in all that Sarah says to you, obey her. . . ." [This is the only verse in the Bible in which a person is told by God to obey a spouse. Interestingly, it was a man who was instructed to obey his wife.]
27:22	The voice is the voice of Jacob, but the hands are the hands of Esau.
42:38	If harm befall him, you will bring down my gray hairs with sorrow to the grave. [Similar to 44:29.]

EXODUS

About 1500 B.C.E.

The Story of Moses

Amram and Yocheved were Levites. Their children were Miriam, Aaron, and Moses.

An edict was issued by Pharaoh to kill all male Hebrew babies. Moses was hidden and then discovered by Pharaoh's daughter, who adopted him.

Moses grew up in the palace but learned from his mother of his Hebrew ancestry.

Moses killed an Egyptian taskmaster and fled to Sinai. He married Tzipora, daughter of Jethro, a Midianite priest, and became a shepherd.

Moses and Tzipora had two sons: Gershom and Eliezer.

The Burning Bush: While herding sheep, Moses saw a bush that appeared to be on fire and was not consumed by the flames. God spoke to him out of the bush.

God told Moses to return to Egypt to save his fellow Hebrews who were suffering under the yoke of slavery. His brother, Aaron, would be his spokesman to Pharaoh.

Moses and Aaron appealed to Pharaoh to allow the Hebrews to go into the wilderness to pray to God. Pharaoh refused and imposed even worse oppression on the Israelites.

Ten Plagues were visited on Egypt: Blood, Frogs, Lice, Insects, Cattle plague, Boils, Hail, Locusts, Darkness, Slaying of the firstborn. With the last plague came the order to leave.

The *first Passover* was celebrated on the eve of the Exodus. At the time the Hebrews ate lamb and matzah; the first because they had sacrificed lambs and used the blood as a sign for the angel of death to *pass over* their homes and the matzah because the bread they baked had not had a chance to rise in their haste to leave Egypt.

About 1450 B.C.E.

The Exodus

Events at the Sea of Reeds (not the Red Sea): The Israelites walked across safely, while the waters closed over the pursuing Egyptians.

Song of the Red Sea is the oldest song of national triumph. Moses and the Israelites praised and thanked God for their escape from Egypt.

Moses took the bones of Joseph to bury them in the Cave of the Machpelah.

The journey through Sinai was filled with crises: The route was circuitous to avoid hostile and marauding tribes and proved not always possible to follow.

The bitter waters at Marah threatened the people with death by thirst in the wilderness. The water was finally sweetened with certain shrubs.

Hunger was abated with manna.

At Rephidim, thirst was again a problem, which was solved by striking the porous rocks that stored water.

The attack of the Amalekites, a predatory tribe that assaulted the weakest and most vulnerable of the Israelites, was subdued by Joshua, Moses' aide, and Hur, his sister's son.

Jethro's visit to Moses in the wilderness: Moses' father-in-law brought Moses his wife and two sons, whom he had left behind when he went back to Egypt.

Jethro gave Moses excellent advice about establishing a system of judges to settle quarrels among the people. This freed him to concentrate on his responsibilities of leadership and enabled the people to secure justice more quickly.

Mount Sinai and the Revelation: Seven weeks after the Exodus the Israelites arrived at Mount Sinai.

Moses ascended Mount Sinai for forty days to receive the Torah from God. Meanwhile, the people built a Golden Calf.

Upon discovering the apostasy, Moses smashed the two tablets of the Law. The people repented and Moses returned to Mount Sinai to receive the tablets again.

The Giving of the Law by God is called the Revelation. It was accompanied by natural phenomena: a thick cloud and smoke, lightning, thunder, earthquake, fire, and the piercing sound of the shofar (ram's horn).

The people accepted the Commandments and promised to obey them.

THE TEN COMMANDMENTS
(EXODUS 20 AND DEUTERONOMY 5)

1. I am the Lord your God who brought you out of the land of Egypt out of the house of slavery.

    The meaning of this commandment is that it is incumbent on Jews to believe:

    There is a deity.

    There is only one God.

    God has a personal interest in mankind.

God has a special relationship to Israel.

God is not equivalent to nature but is over nature.

2. You shall have no other gods besides Me. You shall not make graven images, nor shall you bow down to them.

3. You shall not take the name of the Lord in vain. (Meaning: Do not swear by His name, take it frivolously, or use His ineffable name, for which Jews substitute *Adonai.*)

4. Remember [Observe] the Sabbath and keep it holy.

5. Honor your father and your mother.

6. You shall not murder.

7. You shall not commit adultery.

8. You shall not steal.

9. You shall not bear false witness [lie or slander].

10. You shall not covet your neighbor's wife or possessions.

    (Meaning: Have a predatory desire for what you cannot get honestly.)

Other Laws in the Torah

Following the Ten Commandments are many laws interspersed with narratives of the experiences and challenges the Israelites encountered on their way to the Promised Land. Altogether, the Torah contains 613 laws, 248 of which are positive and 365, negative. They are found mainly in Exodus, Leviticus, Numbers, and Deuteronomy, but there are also some in Genesis.

The laws deal with all aspects of life and include, but are not limited to, such subjects as ethical and moral behavior, special consideration of the weakest members of society (widows, orphans, and poor); prayers and ritual; sanitation and cleanliness; treatment of leprosy and other diseases; quarantine of the sick; considerate behavior toward prisoners and female captives of war; marriage regulations; divorce; punishment for murder and other crimes; Cities of Refuge for accidental killers; Levitical Cities within each of the tribes; observance of Holy Days (Rosh Hashanah and Yom Kippur) and festivals (Passover, Shavuot, Succot); Sabbath observance; mandatory establishment of courts of law; *kashrut* (permitted and forbidden foods); treatment and release of bonded servants; protection of animals; and warning against false prophets and heathen rites.

The Torah also prescribed the construction of the Tabernacle, sometimes called the Tent of Meeting or the Sanctuary. The Israelites carried this tent with them during their forty years in the wilderness and into Canaan or the Land of Israel. It provided a guide to the construction of the Temple in Jerusalem four centuries later.

The Sanctuary or Tabernacle

The two tablets of the Law were kept in the Holy Ark in a special place in the Sanctuary.

Moses communed with God in the Sanctuary.

Aaron, the High Priest, and his descendants prayed in the Holy of Holies in the Sanctuary on Yom Kippur.

Bezalel was the architect of the Sanctuary. Oholiav was the artist who designed its furnishings (curtains, candlesticks, table, altar) and the priests' garments.

Upon completion of the Tabernacle in the wilderness, the Israelites were numbered in a census. There were 603,550 men over age twenty, excluding Levites. This number did not include women or men under twenty years of age. Thus, this assumes a population of 2 million.

The Twelve Tribes of Israel were:[1]

1. Reuben	7. Dan
2. Simeon	8. Asher
3. Judah	9. Gad
4. Issachar	10. Naphtali
5. Zebulun	11. Ephraim
6. Benjamin	12. Manasseh

There is no tribe of Joseph, but he was honored by having tribes named after his two sons, Ephraim and Manasseh.

Famous Verses in Exodus

1:8   There arose a new king over Egypt who knew not Joseph.

3:8   . . . . a land flowing with milk and honey. [Also see 3:17, 13:5. The expression is also found in Leviticus, throughout Numbers and Deuteronomy, and in Joshua, Jeremiah, and Ezekiel.]

19:5   If you will obey Me and keep My Covenant, you will be My own treasure from among all the peoples. [Similar to Deuteronomy 14:2 and 26:18.]

34:6–7   The Lord, the Lord God, merciful and gracious, long-suffering and abundant in goodness and truth; keeping mercy until the thousandth generation, forgiving iniquity, and transgression and sin, and who will not acquit the guilty who are impenitent. [These verses contain the thirteen attributes of God, which He proclaimed to Moses.]

---

1. Levi is not one of the twelve tribes that received land distribution. The Levites served in the Tabernacle and later in the Temple. They were also distributed among the tribes. A branch of the Levites, descended from Aaron, became the priests who had special functions in the Temple ritual.

LEVITICUS

This book consists mostly of ritual laws concerning the priesthood that had been given to Aaron and his sons and their descendants.

The laws of sacrifices include: burnt offerings that showed surrender to God's will; peace offerings that showed gratitude for God's mercies; sin offerings that constituted confession and repentance for wrongdoing; congregational sacrifices that indicated the interdependence of all Israelites.

Instructions to priests regarding sacrifices informed them of their share of the offerings and of their functions in preparing the sacrifices.

Dietary laws stated which animals were permitted (clean); which animals were forbidden (unclean); the ingestion of blood is forbidden.

Laws of leprosy included diagnosis, quarantine, and thorough cleansing before the person returned to society.

Description of what constitutes incestuous marriages: A manual of moral instruction is found in Leviticus, which is listed at the end of the chapter.

Rules of the sabbatical year mandate letting the land lie fallow every seven years.

The Jubilee occurs every fifty years and requires the release of Hebrew slaves; the reversion of property to the original owner; the remission of debts (this was to prevent the concentration of wealth in one group and permanent impoverishment of others).

Famous Verses in Leviticus

Chapter 19 is a manual of moral instruction. Its verses include the following injunctions:

love and respect parents

provide for the poor by not gleaning the corners of the fields and vineyards

be impartial in judgment by not discriminating against the poor or favoring the rich person

love your neighbor as yourself

be respectful to old people

treat the stranger the same way as the citizen by having the same laws for both aliens and natives and do not deceive the former

keep proper and correct weights and measures

Its verses also forbid the following behavior:

worshipping idols

stealing

lying and dealing falsely

oppressing a hired servant; the latter is to be paid his wages on the day of his work

cursing the deaf or putting an obstacle in the way of the blind

talebearing and gossiping, which often leads to slander

standing idly by when one's fellowman is in danger

cutting or mutilating oneself

handing over one's daughter to a man without a legal marriage and thus dishonoring her

NUMBERS

While Leviticus was mostly legislative, Numbers resumes the pattern of Exodus in combining history and law.

About 1450 to 1400 B.C.E.

Numbers continues the narrative of the hardships of the Israelites during the thirty-eight years of their wanderings after the Exodus and Revelation at Sinai.

Additional laws were given, including the Priestly Blessing that has become part of the Jewish and Christian liturgy in their houses of prayer. (See list of famous verses at end of this section.)

A fiery cloud over the tabernacle was a sign of God's presence and also a guide to the Israelites. When the cloud moved, the nation traveled. When the cloud rested, the Hebrews encamped. It was a pillar of cloud by day and of fire by night.

About ten and a half months after their arrival at Sinai, the Hebrews journeyed toward Moab and Israel.

Events in the Wilderness

The Hebrews and the "mixed multitude" (of aliens who had joined the Israelites when they left Egypt) wanted to return to Egypt because of the many hardships:

    chronic shortage of water
    steady diet of manna
    lack of homes
    harsh conditions of life.

The Rebellion at Taberah caused many to be consumed by fire while others died of a plague.

Aaron and Miriam's criticism of Moses because of his marriage (whether to Tzipora or a subsequent wife is not known) resulted in Miriam being stricken with leprosy for her censoriousness.

The Mission of the Twelve Spies sent by Moses was to scout the Promised Land. Ten gave alarming reports that terrified the people. Only Joshua and Caleb assured the people they could succeed.

The Israelites panicked and rebelled. They were condemned to wander in the wilderness for thirty-eight years until the entire older generation died.

Korah rebelled against Moses' leadership, which brought divine execution of him and his supporters.

Moses sinned by striking a rock to extract water instead of talking to it. For this act of impatience, which would have confirmed the miracle, God forbade him to enter the Promised Land.

The defeat of the Amorite kingdoms of Sihon and Og, east of the Jordan River, was the beginning of the conquest of the land.

Final events at Moab, just prior to entering Canaan:

The Story of Balak and Balaam: Balak, king of Moab, hired Balaam, a heathen seer, to curse Israel. He shared the current belief that curses had power to destroy. When he looked down at the Israelites arrayed before him, Balaam was unable to curse them but was compelled to bless them with the famous words "How goodly are your tents, O Jacob

Your dwellings, O Israel" (Numbers 24:5).

The Apostasy of Israelites with Moabites and Midianites caused a plague that killed many Hebrews. The plague stopped when Pinhas, the grandson of Aaron, committed a zealous act; he skewered a Hebrew man and Midianite woman as they lay together.

Joshua was appointed Moses' successor.

The boundaries of Israel were delineated.

Two and a half tribes (Reuben, Gad, and half of Manasseh) were allotted the land east of the Jordan River, where they would settle after all of Canaan was liberated.

Moses' modification of the laws of inheritance assured that a man's landed property would pass on to his daughters in the absence of a male heir, so that the land would not be lost to his descendants.

Famous Verses in Numbers

6:24   The Lord bless you and keep you.

6:25   The Lord make His face shine upon you and be gracious unto you.

6:26   The Lord lift up His countenance upon you and grant you peace.
       [These three verses are the Priestly Blessing well known to Christians and Jews because they are part of the liturgy in their houses of prayer.]

10:35 Rise up, O Lord, and let Your enemies be scattered; and let those who hate You flee before You. [These verses are in the Sabbath liturgy. They are possibly taken from another source, the Book of the Wars of the Lord, which was lost over the centuries. The single scriptural reference to that book is found in Numbers 21:14.]

11:20 . . . you shall eat [meat] until it comes out of your nose.

24:5   How goodly are your tents, O Jacob
       Your dwellings, O Israel.

DEUTERONOMY

This book summarizes much of the previous three books of the Torah. It consists of three farewell addresses by Moses to his people as they prepared to cross the Jordan.

Moses' first speech was a review of Israel's journeys and the events of the past forty years.

Moses' second speech consisted of a review of about thirty previously given laws and the introduction of about seventy new ones.

Moses' third speech affirmed the renewal of the Covenant between God and Israel.

In his last days, Moses concluded his tasks:

He confirmed Joshua as Israel's leader who would lead the nation into Canaan.

He delivered the laws to the priests.

He blessed his people.

Moses ascended Mount Nebo, from where he saw the Promised Land and where he died.

Famous Verses in Deuteronomy

6:4–9 Hear O Israel: The Lord our God, the Lord is One. You shall love the Lord your God with all your heart, and with all your soul, and with all your might. And these words that I command you this day shall be on your heart; you shall teach them diligently to your children and shall talk of them when you sit in the house, when you walk by the way, when you lie down, and when you rise up. You shall bind them for a sign on your hand and as frontlets between your eyes. You shall write them upon the doorposts of your house and upon your gates.

[This has been the watchword and ruling principle of Judaism throughout the ages. It is known as the *Sh'ma* in Hebrew, which is the first word of the prayer.]

7:7–8   The Lord didn't desire you or choose you because you were more numerous than any other people, for you were the fewest of all the peoples; but because the Lord loved you and would keep the oath which He swore to your fathers. . . .

16:19   [Judges] . . . shall not pervert judgment; and not show partiality; nor take a bribe; for a bribe blinds the eyes of the wise and corrupts the words of the righteous.

16:20   Justice, justice shall you follow that you may live and inherit the land which the Lord your God gave you.

24:5   A newly married man shall not be conscripted for war or charged with public duties; he shall be free for his house for one year to cheer his wife.

24:16   The fathers shall not be put to death for the children, and the children shall not be put to death for the fathers. Every man shall be put to death for his own sin.

Tracking the Exodus

There are many theories for tracking the Exodus: a northern route along the Mediterranean called the "Way of the Sea," a central route called the "Way of Shur," and a southern route that passes by Jebel Musa (Mount Moses), the mountain most widely considered Mount Sinai (see Map 1–1).

However, not all archaeologists and scholars agree that Mount Sinai is in the Sinai Peninsula. Professor Frank

Map 1–1 Exodus Routes to Mount Sinai

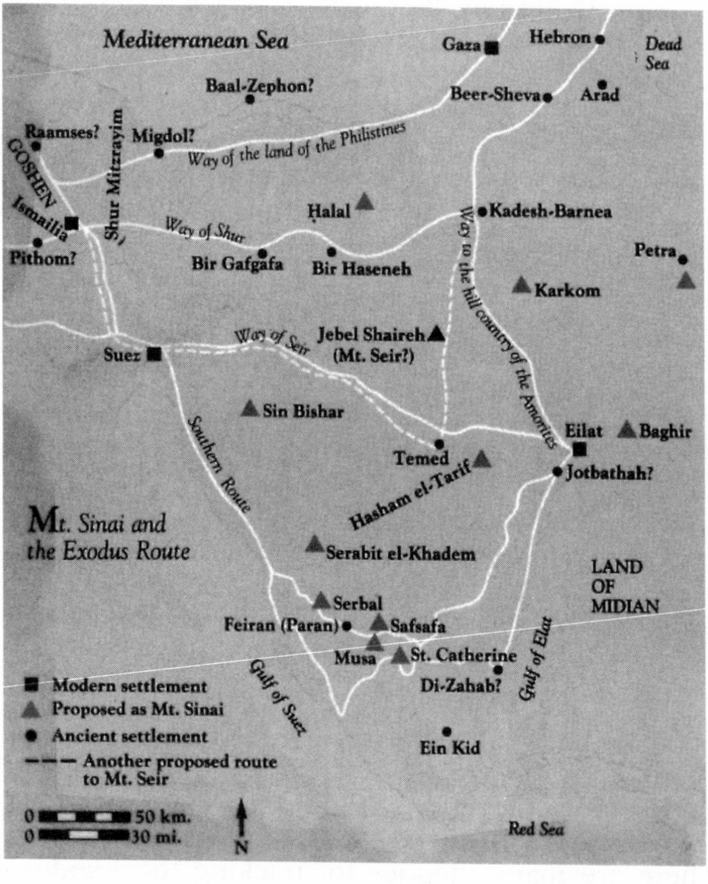

Moore Cross (*Biblical Archaeology Review*, May–June 1988) has postulated that the Israelites desert wanderings occurred in Midian, east of the Gulf of Eilat (northwest Arabia today). There are many mountains in this area. He believes Quaryyah is possibly Mount Sinai. Professor Emmanuel Anati (*Biblical Archaeology Review*,

July–August 1985) places the holy mountain on the Negev–Sinai border, at a site called Har Karkom. The Israelites entered the Promised Land from east of Eilat and the Jordan River.

2

THE EARLY PROPHETS

JOSHUA (CIR. 1400–1350 B.C.E.)

Contents

The Book of Joshua is the natural sequence and conclusion of the Pentateuch, in which are found two central themes: the Revelation of the Torah and the promise to Israel of Canaan (the Land of Israel). The realization of that promise is the substance of this book, which has sometimes been called the "sixth book of the Torah."

According to the Talmud, Joshua wrote this eponymous book and certain passages were then added after his death by the High Priests, Eleazar and Pinhas. The book bears strong evidence of eyewitness accounts of events. Joshua is written in straightforward, historical prose.

The book relates:

1. The conquest of Canaan (the ancient name for Israel)
2. The division of Canaan among the Twelve Tribes of Israel.

3. The spiritual and religious conditions by which the Israelites could win and occupy the land: fidelity to the Torah and observance of its laws.

Narrative

Joshua was appointed Moses' successor.

Joshua reminded the two and a half tribes (Reuben, Gad, and half of Manasseh) that had already received land east of the Jordan River (Trans-Jordan) of their promise to help the other tribes liberate the land west of the Jordan.

Mission of the spies in Jericho was to scout out the land and discover its physical features and defenses.

Rahab sheltered and hid the scouts; she was saved, together with her family, after Israel captured Jericho.

The entire nation crossed the Jordan River with the Ark of the Covenant. The Jordan overflowed its banks and the waters rose in a mass, permitting the people to cross on dry land. This is reminiscent of the crossing of the Red Sea (Sea of Reeds) at the time of the Exodus.

Military conquest of Canaan—tactics and stratagems used:

1. Capture of Jericho—*psychological warfare*: the march around the city walls, with blowing horns and people shouting, resulted in the walls falling down.[1]

---

1. The miraculous nature of this event may have a physical explanation. Soldiers marching across a bridge in formation set up a resonance condition, which can cause steel and concrete in the bridge to vibrate until it collapses. The Israelites marched in formation around the walls of Jericho, setting up a resonance condition which, together with the noise of the horns and shouts of the people, might have caused the mud-brick walls around the city to fall.

2. Capture of Ai—*ambush and attack*: the original battle ended with Israel's defeat due to trespass by Achan, who had taken forbidden spoils of war at Jericho; and overconfidence of the Israelites, who underrated the enemy and attacked with inadequate forces. This was rectified by better planning and preparation.

The battle plan was as follows: Defenders were drawn out of the city by half of Joshua's army; the other half, hidden in ambush, entered the city and burned it. The inhabitants were then caught between the two halves of the Israelite army.

3. Conquest of the South—*surprise attack*: Joshua ordered a forced march in mountainous country by night, which brought his army to its destination unseen and unexpected. Joshua annihilated the five kings who had attacked Gibeon by fighting during the "longest day." ("Sun, stand still upon Gibeon and Moon in the Valley of Ayalon" [Joshua 10:12]).

4. Conquest of the hill country of the north—*bravado*: Joshua led a successful attack on several kings and occupied the land. However, during the period of the Judges, the Canaanites regained control of the territory and oppressed the Israelites.

The land west of the Jordan River was divided among nine and a half tribes.

Geography of the Land Of Israel

The Jordan River divides the country in two parts (see Map 2–1).

WEST OF THE JORDAN

Shephala—lowlands; the seacoast running the length of the country on the west.

Map 2–1 Ancient Israel and Surrounding Nations, Including Edom, Moab, Ammon, Phoenicia, and Damascus (Aram)

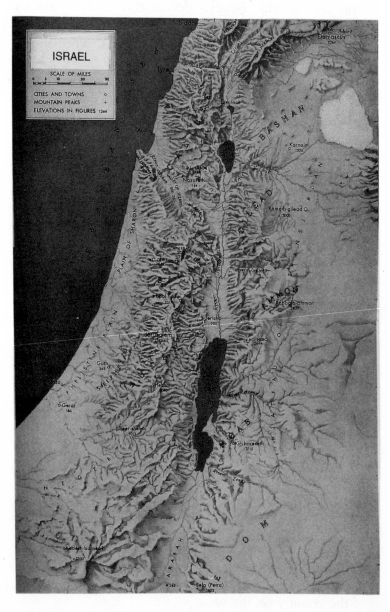

Har—hill country or mountains running down the center of the country from north to south.

Aravah—plain or valley of the Jordan River, both north and south of the Dead Sea.

Negev—dry land south of Judah and Beersheba.

EAST OF THE JORDAN

Bashan—north of the Yarmuk River to Syria; called the Golan today.

Gilead—from the Yarmuk to the Yabbok River.

Emek—from the Yabbok River south to the Arnon River.

After the land was divided and the tribes were settled, the following cities were set aside in their territories.

Six Cities of Refuge were set aside for accidental killers to escape the blood vengeance of the victims' families. The cities were accessible from every part of the country.

Kadesh in Galilee (Naphtali)   Golan in Bashan
                                                        (Manasseh)
Shechem in Samaria (Ephraim)   Ramot in Gilead (Gad)
Hebron in Judah   Bezer in South Trans-
                                                        Jordan (Reuben)

Forty-eight Levitical Cities were set aside for the Tribe of Levi, which did not get any territory. The Levites were to serve religious functions among their fellow Israelites and were, therefore, distributed throughout Israel.

Ten cities within the territory of Judah were allotted to the tribe of Simeon.

Joshua's farewell addresses:

1. Reminded the people of all God had done for them in the Exodus, during the wandering in the wilderness, and in the conquest of Canaan.
2. Warned Israel to keep its faith or it, too, would be driven out of the land.
3. Reminded the nation that there was still more land to be liberated in Canaan.

Joshua was buried in Shechem.

Famous Verses in Joshua

1:6   Be strong and of good courage. [This verse was repeated in 1:7, 9, 18, and 10:25. It may have become a watchword in the time of Joshua to encourage the nation. In modern times the phrase has been used as a greeting and slogan among certain parties or groups.]

1:8   This book of the law shall not depart from you, but you shall meditate on it day and night to do all that is written; for then you will be prosperous and successful.

10:12   Sun, stand still upon Gibeon;
        And moon in the Valley of Ayalon.

10:13   And the sun stood still and the moon stayed
        Until the nation had avenged itself of its enemies.

JUDGES (CIR. 1350–1060 B.C.E.)

Contents

This book continues the story of how the Twelve Tribes of Israel became the Nation of Israel. It deals with the period from the death of Joshua (about 1350) to the birth of Samuel (about 1060). The historical events have an authenticity in that they are told as though from first hand information.

During this period, individual tribes or groups of tribes fought off various hostile nations that surrounded them. These nations attacked the Israelites and subjugated them. They were a threat to the Israelites both physically and morally, as the Hebrews were often attracted to their gods, their idol worship, and their heathen customs.

The judges were military and political leaders who led the Israelites in battle against their oppressors. The judges also governed the people and kept them faithful to the laws of the Torah.

The surrounding nations that Israel fought and eventually conquered were: Ammon, Moab, Edom, Midian, Aram, Jebus, Philistia, and the Canaanites (see Map 2–2).

Author and Date

The book is anonymous. Tradition has ascribed it to Samuel. The style is clear and historical, similar to that found in the books of Samuel.

Map 2–2 Map of Israel during the Period of the Judges

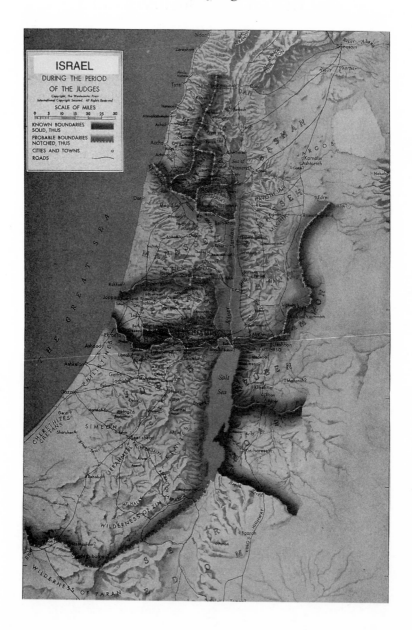

Narrative

After Joshua's death there was recurring backsliding by the Israelites. They were faithless to God and Torah as they worshipped various heathen gods: Baal, Ashtoreth, Moloch, and Chemosh.

Paganism weakened the bonds among the tribes and led to disunity. It became easier to attack, defeat, and subjugate the tribes.

Whenever Israel fell into the hands of other nations and suffered, the people cried to God in remorse. A judge would then rise to redeem them.

MAJOR JUDGES

Name	Tribe	Oppressing Power	Their Leader
Othniel	Judah	Aram (Syria)	Cushan-Rishataim
Ehud	Benjamin	Moab	Eglon

When bringing tribute to Eglon, Ehud found a pretext to be alone with him and killed him. He fled across the Jordan and mobilized the Israelites. Without their king, the Moabites were psychologically undermined and unprepared for battle; they were defeated.

Deborah	Ephraim	Hazor (N. Canaan)	Yavin

Barak, an Israelite general, insisted that Deborah accompany him, even though she advised him that the victory would be credited to a woman. Sisera, a Canaanite general, fled the battlefield.

Yael, a Kenite woman alone in her tent, had the courage to kill Sisera when he sought refuge with her.

The Song of Deborah recounts Israel's victory.

Name	Tribe	Oppressing Power
Gideon	Manasseh	Midian

Gideon demanded proof from an angel sent by God that he was selected to be a judge who would lead Israel to victory.

Tactics in battle: a small army of 300 men (who were selected out of an original 32,000) carried horns, pitchers, and torches. A night attack on the Midianite camp resulted in its complete rout.

Gideon had seventy sons, one of whom, Abimelech, was by his concubine in Shechem.

Abimelech intrigued to become ruler in Shechem and then murdered all his brothers except Yotam, who escaped.

Yotam's fable about the trees (olive, fig, vine, and bramble) was a parable, which inspired the people to overthrow Abimelech.

Jephtha	Gilead (E. Manasseh)	Ammon

At first rejected by his half brothers, Jephtha was asked by them to lead them in battle.

Jephtha's tragic vow regarding his daughter, should he be victorious, led to personal misfortune, the exact nature of which is unclear.

Jephtha took stern military action against the Ephraimites. The latter threatened his tribe for not inviting them to join in battle against Ammon.

Samson	Dan	Philistia

Nazirite by birth (no haircut or intoxicating drinks).

Marriage to Philistine woman in Timna who betrayed the secret of his riddle.

Supernatural strength and exploits against the Philistines.

Infatuation with Delilah in Sorek and her betrayal of him.

Samson's revenge against the Philistines and his death at the temple of Dagon.

Samson was the last judge and an exception to their high standard. He himself never claimed to be a judge. Nor did he deliver Israel from the Philistines. However, in his final act, Samson killed thousands of Philistines, including their leaders.

The remaining chapters in Judges deal with various episodes:

Micah, an Ephraimite, made an idol, built a shrine and appointed a Levite to serve as a priest in it.

The tribe of Dan, unable to hold the territory between Judah and Philistia, found another territory, Laish, in north Israel, which they conquered and settled. These Danites took Micah's idol and kidnapped his priest to serve them.

The concubine of a Levite was raped and murdered at Gibeah by Benjaminites. The Levite cut up her body into twelve pieces, which he sent to all the tribes with an account of the outrage. This resulted in a war against Benjamin and a ban on marriages with that tribe by the other tribes. This policy was eventually reversed in order to prevent the extinction of the tribe.

The Book of Judges closes with a comment that recognized that its final period was a lawless time in Israel, for "every man did that which was right in his own eyes" (Judges 21:25).

1, 2 SAMUEL (CIR. 1060–970 B.C.E.)

Samuel was the most influential and dominant character of his age. He was a judge, prophet, and priest. Samuel was the last of the judges, the first prophet after Moses, and came from a priestly family. He was also a statesman and kingmaker, having chosen the first two kings of Israel: Saul and David.

The Book of 1 Samuel continues the account of the period of the judges until the establishment of the monarchy under Saul. The book ends with the death of Saul, which followed Samuel's passing.

The Book of 2 Samuel is concerned with the career of King David and events during his rule.

1 Samuel

Samuel's parents:

Elkanah and Hannah;
Hannah had long been barren; she prayed fervently for a
    son at the Sanctuary at Shilo, where the Ark of the
    Covenant was kept;
Eli was the priest at Shilo.

Samuel's birth:

Dedicated to the service of the Lord by his mother;
Grew up at Shilo with Eli;
God's call came to Samuel as a child;
God's continued appearance to Samuel established him
    as a prophet.

The great disaster:

Philistines defeated Israel and dominated the country for
the next fifty years;
Ark of the Covenant was taken by the Philistines and
presaged the death of Eli and his sons;
Shilo ceased to be the central sanctuary;
Philistines afflicted with sickness wherever the Ark was
brought;
The Ark was returned to Israel, but there was no longer
a central place of worship. It was kept at Kiriat Yearim
until the Temple was built;
Samuel admonished Israel to be faithful to their God and
cease their heathen practices.

People demanded a king:

Need for a leader in time of war to unite the nation;
Samuel was old and the people did not want his corrupt
sons to lead them;
Samuel was displeased and opposed a monarch.
Warned about the demands a king would make on them,
such as military service, taxation, and forced labor. (1
Samuel 8:10–18).
The people nonetheless insisted on a king.

Saul chosen as king of Israel:

Samuel's meeting with Saul: a young, tall, imposing figure, he was a modest shepherd from Benjamin, the
smallest tribe.
Saul, anointed king by Samuel, was then chosen by lot
by the people.
Saul proved his worth in military victories against Israel's
enemies and oppressors:

1. Saul defeated the Ammonites in defense of Gilead against their humiliating demands;
2. Saul started the war of liberation against the Philistines;
3. Saul defeated Edom, Zobah, and Amalek.

Samuel's constant criticism and rebuke of Saul throughout his reign undermined his self-confidence and position as king. This placed a burden of emotional distress and mental anguish on Saul, possibly causing his depressions and psychotic episodes. Samuel even anointed David king while Saul was still the monarch, thus increasing Saul's insecurity and justifying his fears.

David

He was the youngest of seven sons of Jesse and came from the tribe of Judah. He was charismatic, handsome, brave, a natural leader, and a successful warrior. He was a musician who played the harp and a poet who wrote psalms. He was also an adulterer who ordered the death of an innocent man whose wife he had seduced. He had at least seven or eight wives and an unknown number of concubines. He fathered at least nineteen sons and one daughter, Tamar.

He was originally brought to Saul to play for him when the latter fell into a deep depression.

Story of David and Goliath

The Philistine giant taunted the Israelites and dared them to send a man to fight him. The winner would determine which nation was victorious. David successfully answered Goliath's challenge. The Philistines thereupon fled.

The people praised David over Saul for his military prowess.

David and Jonathan

There was a strong bond of friendship between David and Saul's son. Jonathan's unselfish devotion saved David's life more than once.

David married Saul's daughter, Michal.

Saul's jealousy of David and melancholic depression led him to attempts on his life. David had several escapes:

1. Fled from Saul's spear while playing for him.
2. Saved by Michal's trick and deception of her father.
3. Took refuge with Samuel.
4. Warned by Jonathan of danger from his father.
5. Escaped to Nob, where the High Priest, Ahimelech, gave him food and a sword. (Saul ordered the priests to be massacred for this act.)
6. Flight to Gath, a Philistine city; pretended madness.
7. Escape to Cave of Adullum.

David attracted a force of 600 loyal fighting men. He spared Saul's life while the latter was in pursuit of him.

Samuel died and was mourned throughout Israel.

Episode concerning David and Abigail, Nabal's wife: Abigail appeased David by providing food for him and his army against her husband's wishes. Nabal died of a stroke when he learned what she had done. David, thereupon, married her.

Major battle between Israel and the Philistines:

David's dubious position among the Philistines;

Saul's resort to necromancy: the Witch of Endor summoned Samuel's spirit, which foretold the defeat of

Israel and the deaths of Saul and three of his sons,
including Jonathan;
Bodies of Saul and his sons were retrieved by men of
Gilead and given an honorable burial.

2 Samuel

David was informed of Saul's death. His lament over
Saul and Jonathan is a beautiful elegy.

David had been anointed king by Samuel privately,
about five and a half years earlier, *while Saul ruled as
king.* After Saul's death, he had a public ceremony and
was accepted as king by the men of his tribe, Judah.

His military leaders were his nephews: Joab, Avishai,
and Assael, the sons of his sister, Zeruyah.

Ish-boshet, Saul's remaining son, was anointed king
of Israel by his general, Abner.

Civil war broke out between the Houses of David and
Saul. Assael provoked a fight with Abner and was killed
by him. A quarrel developed between Ish-boshet and
Abner. Abner negotiated with David to bring over all of
Israel to David in exchange for replacing Joab. Joab
killed Abner to eliminate competition and revenge his
brother's death. Ish-boshet was assassinated by his own
people. Israel did not want to prolong the struggle with
Judah, especially since both the king and military leader
were dead.

David was anointed king over all Israel at Hebron.
He was thirty when he became king of Judah. He ruled
from Hebron seven and a half years and from Jerusalem, thirty-three years.

David's children: six sons were born to him in Hebron.
Amnon, Daniel (or Chileab), Absolom, Adoniyah, Sheph-

atiah, and Itream. In Jerusalem, eleven more sons were born to him, the fourth being Solomon.

David's great military successes and other accomplishments:

1. He gave the final crushing defeat to the Philistines, which freed Israel from all further danger and domination by them;
2. Captured Jerusalem from the Jebusites: city strategically located and difficult to conquer; geographically centered between Judah and Israel;
3. Built a palace in Jerusalem;
4. Transferred the Ark from Kiriat Yearim to Jerusalem, but was forbidden to build the Temple;
5. Extended the boundaries of Israel and protected its frontiers by defeating Moab, Aram, Edom, Ammon, and Amalek;
6. David was kind to Mephiboshet, Jonathan's son, who was lame, thus keeping a promise he had made to Jonathan.

David sinned with Bathsheba, wife of Uriah, the Hittite. A plot by David and Joab to prevent the exposure of the sin led to Uriah's death. Bathsheba became David's wife. The prophet Nathan confronted David with a parable about his wrongdoing. David and Bathsheba's illicitly conceived child died. Bathsheba subsequently bore Solomon, who is listed as her fourth son.

Strife in David's family: Amnon, David's oldest son, raped Tamar, his half sister. David's failure to castigate Amnon led Absolom to avenge his sister by killing Amnon. Absolom's flight, prolonged absence, and rejection by David led to his eventual revolt.

Absolom's revolt against David to replace him on the throne:

ABSOLOM

Amasa was his general
Ahitophel, his advisor

DAVID

Joab, his nephew, was his ever-loyal general
Zadok and Aviathar were his loyal priests
Hushai, a faithful servant, counteracted Ahitophel's advice
to David, which was beneficial to Absolom and harm-
ful to David.

Ahitophel's suicide was one of the few in the Bible,
after he realized that "his side" had lost and that he
would be subject to David's revenge.

David won a complete victory. Joab killed Absolom,
an act expressly forbidden by David. David's grief was
expressed in his poignant lament, "My son, my son"
(2 Samuel 19:5).

Amasa was given the command of David's forces
after Absolom's death but failed to fulfill his first mission, to quell a rebellion promptly. He was murdered
by Joab.

David's Census: David ordered a census in violation
of laws prohibiting the numbering of Israel, except at
divine command (Numbers 1:1–3, 3:14–15, 26:1–2).
David's sin brought severe punishment to the nation in
the form of a plague causing a great loss of life.

The book concludes with a hymn of thanksgiving and
a psalm.

1, 2 KINGS (CIR. 970–586 B.C.E.)

The Books of Kings continue the history of the monarchy begun in the Books of Samuel. Kings records the end of David's reign and succession of his son, Solomon, up to the time of the Babylonian captivity.

The Temple, Prophets, and Davidic Dynasty (descendants of David on the throne of Israel or Judah) were the outward signs of God's presence among His people.

The purpose of the books is the moral and spiritual instruction contained therein. The historical events are a means of teaching and proving the importance of devotion to the one God, the practice of justice, and adherence to the laws of His Torah. This applies to both king and commoner. As long as Solomon was righteous, all went well for him. However, when he deviated into permitting idolatry in his kingdom and, indeed, in his household, he suffered divine retribution. The same applied to the nation of Israel, as a whole. The message of Kings and all the prophetic books was that obedience brought national security and prosperity, while idolatry led to national calamity, which culminated in exile.

The Book of 1 Kings tells the history from the end of David's reign through Solomon's reign and recounts the events leading to the Divided Kingdom of Judah and Israel. The book records episodes during the sovereignty of the first four kings of Judah from Rehoboam through Jehosaphat. It also describes the establishment of the Kingdom of Israel under Jeroboam and tells about his successors through the reign of Ahab.

The Book of 2 Kings continues the history of each kingdom: Judah in the south and Israel in the north. The book follows the dynasties of the remaining kings in Israel until its fall in 721 to Assyria and the exile of its people. The events in the history of Judah under its kings from Jehosaphat to Zedekiah are recounted up to the defeat and exile of Judah in 586 by Babylonia.

1 Kings

Last Days of David's Reign

1. Adoniyah, David's fourth son and the one next in succession to the throne, was displaced by Solomon through the intrigues of the following: his mother, Bathsheba; the High Priest, Zadok; Nathan the prophet; and Benaya, head of David's personal guard.
2. Solomon was proclaimed king; Adoniyah submitted to him.
3. Solomon given the last charge and instructions by David: find a pretext to kill Joab. Despite the general's eternal loyalty to David, the latter never forgave him for killing Absolom. Solomon was to reward Barzillai, who had brought David food during his battle against Absolom.

The Glories and Apostasy of Solomon's Reign

1. Solomon removed all his adversaries and possible rivals: had his brother, Adoniyah, killed; banished Aviathar, the High Priest who had supported Adoniyah.
2. Solomon had power, wealth, and fame and was considered wise and pious. He built the Temple in Jerusalem. He was visited by the Queen of Sheba (its location could be southwest Arabia, Ethiopia, or Egypt).

3. He married foreign women and built temples and altars to their gods. Solomon imposed economic strain on his people to support such luxury. He was too distracted to subdue other nations that rose against him. His empire was torn away from his son, and the nation was divided.

The Divided Monarchy

Rehoboam (932–916) crowned king; acted unwisely toward representative of the northern tribes when they appealed to him for tax relief.

Jeroboam (932–912) led the revolt of the northern tribes and established the Kingdom of Israel, which consisted of *nine* tribes: Zebulun, Issachar, Asher, Naphtali, Dan, Manasseh, Ephraim, Reuben, and Gad.

The kingdom of Judah consisted of that tribe and Benjamin, *plus Simeon*. The latter was assigned land within the tribe of Judah and eventually merged with that tribe. Simeon lost its separate identity. Consequently, when the country split into two kingdoms, the southern was known as the kingdom of two tribes (namely, Judah and Benjamin), not three.

Jeroboam set up altars for the worship of golden calves in the north so that the people would not go to the Temple in Jerusalem. The centers of religious worship (Temple in Judah and altars in Israel) served as unifying forces.

Rehoboam of Judah also sinned with heathen worship (which he had grown up with).

Shishak of Egypt attacked Jerusalem and plundered the Temple.

Series of Kings in Israel and Judah

(See also the chronological table at the end of this chapter.)

Asa of Judah (932–916) was a righteous king; showed loyalty to God by destroying idols during his reign. Asa made a pact with Ben-hadad of Aram (Syria) against Baasha, king of Israel.

Baasha of Israel (911–888) murdered Jeroboam's family. He and his successors continued the idolatry that Jeroboam had started. His dynasty lasted for fifty-seven years, until one of his descendants was assassinated.

Omri (887–876) built the city of Samaria and established it as the capital of Israel.

Ahab's reign in Israel (876–855) was particularly wicked: Married Jezebel; erected altars to Baal to please her. Permitted the murder of Navot to acquire his vineyard. Wars with Ben-hadad of Aram resulted in his ignominious death. Tolerated Jezebel's false prophets.

Prophet Elijah (first half of the ninth century) performed his miraculous deeds: provided food for a poor widow and saved her son's life; challenged the prophets of Baal on Mount Carmel, where his offering was accepted. Fearless stand against Ahab, Jezebel, and the false prophets of Baal. Flight to Judah for safety.

2 Kings

Appointment of Elisha, in accordance with God's command, to succeed Elijah as leading prophet. Elijah's farewell and ascent to heaven. Elisha's mission was in the second half of ninth century.

Jehosaphat's reign in Judah ((874–850) was righteous, like that of his father, Asa.

Reign of *Yoram* of Israel, son of Ahab (854–843). Conquest and destruction of Moab by an alliance of Israel, Judah, and Edom against Mesha, king of Moab.

Elisha's miraculous acts: purified the water of Jericho, provided oil for a poor widow; assured a Shunemite woman she would have a child, and later saved the child's life with mouth-to-mouth resuscitation; cured Naaman, a Syrian general, of leprosy.

Siege of Samaria and famine. Sudden and miraculous end of the siege and the famine, as Elisha predicted. As also predicted by Elisha, Ben-hadad was replaced by Hazael on the Syrian throne. He was cruel and treacherous to Israel.

Reign of *Yoram* of Judah, son of Jehosaphat (850–843). Yoram married Athaliah, sister of Yoram of Israel and daughter of Ahab and Jezebel. Like her mother, she was a bad influence on her husband. Yoram's son, *Ahaziah*, succeeded him and then died, after a one-year reign.

Yehu (843–816) anointed king of Israel by one of Elisha's prophets. He killed Yoram of Israel and Ahaziah of Judah while they were engaged in battle against Hazael of Syria. He also killed Jezebel. He had all Ahab's descendants murdered. He destroyed Baal worship and killed its followers. Israel lost territory east of the Jordan to Syria.

Athaliah (842–837) seized the throne of Judah after her son, Ahaziah, was killed. She murdered all the male members of the royal family except Yoash, who was saved and hidden by his sister for six years. Yehoyada, a priest, plotted the overthrow of Athaliah. Athaliah was executed.

Reign of *Yoash* of Judah (837–798): Yoash became king at the age of seven. He restored the Temple and improved the system of collection for its upkeep. Hazael threatened Jerusalem. Yoash bribed him with Temple treasure to avoid attack. His servants conspired against him and killed him.

Yehoahaz (816–800) and *Yoash* (800–785) of Israel, son and grandson of Yehu. Oppression by the Syrians was followed by successes of Israel against them after Israel repented and asked God's help. Death of Elisha.

Amaziah's reign in Judah (798–790): he took vengeance on the murderers of his father, Yoash. Conquered Edom. Made a rash challenge to Yoash of Israel and was defeated by him. The king of Israel destroyed part of the protecting wall around Jerusalem and took treasure from the Temple. Amaziah was murdered in a conspiracy.

Jeroboam II (785–745) and *Zechariah* (745) were the third and fourth generations of Yehu's descendants on Israel's throne. With them Yehu's dynasty ended. Religious backsliding from Yehu's reforms. Israel first lost and then regained land taken by Syria.

Azariah, also known as Uzziah, of Judah (790–739): was a righteous king; abolished heathen practices. The "Earthquake of Uzziah" occurred in 747 during his reign. He was afflicted with leprosy, supposedly for a sacrilegious act. His son, *Yotam*, was also a good king. Isaiah's mission started at the end of Azariah's reign and continued through the reigns of three more kings of Judah: Yotam, Ahaz, and Hezekiah.

Last kings of Israel: *Shallum, Menahem, Pekahiah, Pekah, and Hoshea* (745–722). All were murdered by their successors except Menahem and Hoshea, who had no successor. Assyria began its rise as a world power at this time: about 745. Tiglath-pileser III of Assyria attacked Israel during Menahem's reign (745–736). Menahem became his vassal and paid tribute to Assyria through public taxation.

Yotam (739–735) and *Ahaz* (735–720), kings of Judah: Israel allied itself with Syria against Judah. Ahaz secured aid from Assyria for this joint attack. Ahaz despoiled the Temple to bribe Assyria for its help and introduced heathen practices.

End of the Kingdom of Israel

In 722 the Assyrians, under Shalmaneser and then under Sargon, conquered Israel, destroyed Samaria, took Hoshea prisoner, and sent the Israelites into captivity (exile). In addition, they colonized the land of Israel with foreign settlers.

The Kingdom of Israel ceased to exist by 721. The people of the northern tribes who did not escape to Judah were scattered and, for the most part, lost. Remnants of those tribes have been found in various parts of the world, such as Ethiopia and India.

A mixed cult came into being, which consisted of people from various lands who were settled in Samaria. They were called Samaritans, or *Shomronim* in Hebrew.

The biblical interpretation of the catastrophe stated that exile was the result of, and punishment for, disregarding the Torah, neglecting the worship of God, and adopting heathen rites and practices.

A secular explanation is that the Israelites, in adopting the customs and values of the surrounding nations, had no distinguishing beliefs to defend. They lost their unique identity and had nothing to fight for. Thus they fell victim to the heathen nations to whom they had assimilated.

The Surviving Kingdom of Judah

Hezekiah (720–687) was one of the best and greatest kings of Judah, although he was the son and father of evil kings, Ahaz and Manasseh, respectively. Faithful to God and Torah, he initiated religious reforms that eliminated idolatrous practices.

Hezekiah's tunnel, a marvel of ancient engineering, protected the water supply for the population in the event of siege by bringing the waters of Gihon Spring inside the Jerusalem walls.

Judah enjoyed great material prosperity during Hezekiah's reign.

Judah revolted against Assyria. Sennacherib invaded Judah and threatened to destroy Jerusalem.

Hezekiah's fervent prayer for Jerusalem's safety was answered by a miraculous destruction of Sennacherib's army. A total of 185,000 soldiers were suddenly slain before they could attack or besiege Jerusalem.

The reigns of *Manasseh* (687–638) and *Amon* (638–637): they reversed Hezekiah's reforms and revived idolatry. Superstition and immorality were rampant.

The reign of *Josiah* (637–607) was accompanied by a religious reformation. While repairs were made on the Temple, the "Book of the Law" was discovered; this was probably Deuteronomy. Idolatrous places of worship were destroyed. People were called to hear the Law read and to celebrate Passover. Josiah fell in battle against Pharaoh Necco II.

The Last Kings of Judah

Yehoahaz (607), Josiah's son, fought against Egypt. He was deposed by Egypt and replaced by his brother, *Yehoyakim* (607–597), who was put on the throne as a vassal of Egypt.

Babylonia rose to power. Nebuchadnezzar defeated Egypt and took over Judah. Yehoyakim rebelled against Nebuchadnezzar and was killed. *Yehoyachin*, his son, became king but ruled only three months.

The End of the Kingdom of Judah

Nebuchadnezzar captured Jerusalem in 597. Yehoyachin, along with his family, ministers, officers, leaders, and all skilled craftsmen, was exiled to Babylonia. Yehoyachin was imprisoned. There were 10,000 exiles in the first captivity. The wealth of the Temple and palace was looted.

Zedekiah, Josiah's third son, was the last king of Judah. He was on the throne from 597 to 586. He rebelled against Babylonia; his sons were killed and he was taken prisoner to Babylonia where he died.

Destruction of the Temple and Jerusalem

The second Babylonian captivity occurred in 586 (see Map 2–3). Gedaliah was appointed governor and was treacherously murdered. The remnant of the Jews fled to Egypt.

In 562 Nebuchadnezzar died. His successor released Yehoyachin after thirty-five years and treated him honorably. A descendant of David, Yehoyachin (also called

Map 2–3 The Route of the Judean Exiles
to Babylonia

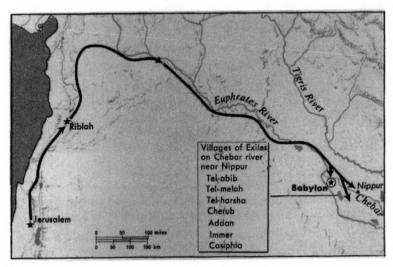

Yeconiah), survived after he was released from prison
by the Babylonians. That a descendant of David was
still alive gave hope that the captivity would end and
the exiles would return to Judah.

CHRONOLOGICAL TABLE OF THE KINGS
OF JUDAH AND ISRAEL
United Kingdom

Saul, 1030–1006 B.C.E.
David, 1011–971
Solomon, 971–932

Divided Kingdom

Judah		Israel	
932–916	Rehoboam	Jeroboam	932–912
916–914	Aviyam		
914–874	Asa	Nadav	912–911
		Baasha	911–888
		Elah*	888–887
		Zimri (7 days)*	887
		Omri	887–876
874–850	Jehosaphat	Ahab	876–855
		Ahaziah	855–854
850–843	Yoram	Yoram*	854–843
843–842	Ahaziah*	Yehu	843–816
842–837	Athaliah*		
837–798	Yoash*	Yehoahaz	816–800
798–790	Amaziah*	Yoash	800–785
790–739	Azariah (Uzziah)	Jeroboam II	785–745
		Zechariah (6 mos.)*	745
		Shallum (1 mo.)*	745
739–735	Yotam	Menahem	745–736
		Pekahiah*	736–735
735–720	Ahaz	Pekah*	735–732
		Hoshea	732–722
720–687	Hezekiah		
687–638	Manasseh		
638–637	Amon		
637–607	Josiah		
607 (3 mos.)	Yehoahaz		
607–597	Yehoyakim		
597 (3 mos)	Yehoyachin		
597–586	Zedekiah		

Note: All kings of Israel were considered wicked in the Bible because they set up pagan sanctuaries where idolatry was practiced. They did this to divert the Israelites from the Temple in Jerusalem and to create a religious cohesion among them. The following kings of Judah were considered good and righteous in the Bible: Asa, Jehosaphat, Azariah, Yotam, Hezekiah, and Josiah.

*Assassinated

3

THE LATER PROPHETS

The Later Prophets include Isaiah, Jeremiah, Ezekiel, and the Twelve "Minor" Prophets.

The prophets were considered divinely inspired people whose messages to the Israelites had a threefold purpose:

1. To rebuke the people for their backsliding and wrongdoing and prod them to change their behavior.
2. To warn the nation of punishment for continued sinfulness and immorality and to assure the people of forgiveness if they relented and changed their ways.
3. To console the nation, after national calamity had occurred (such as the destruction of their land and exile), that the people would return to their homeland, rebuild it, live in peace, and remain God's people.

Biblical prophecy typically dealt with contemporary, prevailing conditions and predictions about the *near* future. Prophets often spoke of events that would occur within a period of twenty years or less. Occasionally, they foretold events happening fifty to seventy years into the future. However, the Hebrew prophets did not deal with prognostications about the distant future. That is the area of apocalyptic writers like Daniel.

The behavior that the prophets condemned was no worse than that of the surrounding nations. In fact, the leaders of the peoples mentioned in the Bible with whom Israel had contact had no limits or controls on their exploitation of the poor. There were no laws restricting the absolute power of the king, nobility, and priests over their subordinates. In Israel there was a body of laws, the Torah, which was, at least theoretically, acknowledged by everyone. These laws were incumbent on everyone, from the king on down. They guaranteed the people the right to the fruits of their labor and protection against arbitrary cruelty. Moreover, only in Israel did there arise prophets who harangued and threatened the monarchs, nobles, priests, and wealthy for their violation of those laws.

ISAIAH (PROPHETIC MISSION CIR. 740–687 B.C.E.)

Personal Background

His name means "help (or salvation) of God." It reflects Isaiah's teachings and hopes.

Isaiah's mission lasted from about 740 to 687 B.C.E. in Jerusalem during the sovereignty of four kings: toward the end of Azariah's rule and throughout the reigns of Yotam, Ahaz, and Hezekiah. He died during the reign of the wicked Menashe.

He was a prophet, statesman, and orator. He was a deeply religious man in terms of holding high ethical standards. He was a statesman who understood the political world around him. He knew the conditions of the common people as well as of the aristocracy, from which he came.

Historical Events during Isaiah's Mission

Isaiah lived during one of the most critical periods in the history of Israel. Egypt and Assyria were the two world powers; the former was declining and the latter was rising. Israel was caught between the two geographically.

735   Syria and Israel invaded Judah.* Isaiah assured King Ahaz that both invading countries would be destroyed by Assyria.

732   Syria (called Aram) fell.

---

*Judah is the same as Judea.

722   Israel (also called the Northern Kingdom, Samaria, and Ephraim) fell. Sargon of Assyria invaded, conquered, and exiled the northern tribes. They disappeared as a nation, although many individuals escaped to Judah.

720   King Hezekiah ruled over the northern territory of Israel. For the first time since 932, the lands of Israel and Judah were united under one king.

701   Assyria invaded Judah and ravaged many cities. Hezekiah paid tribute to Assyria. For the next fourteen years he built up the Judean defenses and strongholds. He allied himself with Tirhaka of Ethiopia and revolted against Assyrian domination.

687   Sennacherib brought his army to war against Jerusalem. His general, Ravsheka, warned the Judeans (Jews)* to capitulate or be destroyed, as Israel had been. On the night of Passover, 687, Sennacherib's army of 185,000 men suddenly died (and/or fled) in a consuming blast before the walls of Jerusalem as they were prepared to attack. The cause of annihilation could have been a cosmic episode occurring at a fortuitous time and interpreted as a miracle. Thus, Jerusalem and Judah were saved for another century.

Composition of the Book

There are sixty-six chapters, which can be divided into three time periods as follows:

Chapters 1 through 39 are called First Isaiah. These are considered the writings of Isaiah of Jerusalem, covering the period from about 740 to 687 B.C.E.

---

*Jews is another word for Judeans.

Chapters 40 through 55 are called Second (or Deutero-) Isaiah and cover the period of the Babylonian exile.

Chapters 56 through 66 are called Third or (Trito-) Isaiah and are postexilic writings.

The traditional view holds that Isaiah of Jerusalem wrote the entire book.

Style and Diction

As one of the greatest orators of all time, Isaiah used picturesque language and powerful figures of speech, as seen in the following examples:

Metaphor: Filth and blood representing the sins of the people would be washed away when they repented

Parable: Vineyard that was cared for and gave forth wild grapes, as God cared for Israel

Allegory: I raised sons and they rebelled against me, as God and Israel

Symbolism: Daughter of Zion is left like a hut in the field, representing Israel abandoned

Assonance: Read in Hebrew 5:7, 22:5

Isaiah's Pronouncement on Israel's Neighbors

Assyria, which had exiled Israel, would be overthrown by Babylonia.

Philistia, Moab, Syria, Egypt, Edom, and Phoenicia (Tyre and Sidon) had oppressed Israel and warred against her. All would meet with national calamities.

Babylonia, which would eventually destroy Jerusalem and Judah and send the Jews into exile, would itself be destroyed and conquered by Persia.

Moral, Religious, and National Teachings of Isaiah

1. Denounced immoral conditions in Judah such as idolatry, superstition, greed of the rich, bribery of judges, adultery, and drunkenness.
2. Declared that without ethical behavior, outward ritual observances such as sacrifices, fasts, prayers, and attendance at sanctuaries are worthless and meaningless.
3. Condemned exploitation of the weak—the poor, widowed, and orphaned—and corruption and injustice among the rich and powerful.
4. Warned that the acceptance of idolatry and heathen customs of the surrounding nations would dilute the religion and faith of Israel and thus weaken the nation.
5. Taught that the only salvation for Israel was a return to the laws of the Torah and reliance on God.
6. Warned against alliances with surrounding nations: Egypt, Syria, and Assyria.

God and Israel

There is a special, everlasting relationship between God and Israel.

God chose Israel to bring His message (Torah) to all the nations.

Israel is God's people; He may chasten them, but never annihilate them.

Although the Lord is God of Israel in a special sense, He is the Universal Sovereign of all mankind. He is not limited to one nation.

The Servant of God (52:13–53:12) ("the Suffering Servant") is a personification of the ideal Israel or the faithful remnant that suffered martyrdom and will ultimately triumph. *The servant is a symbol of the nation and not an individual.*

Visions of the Future or Prophecies of the Messianic Age

The Messianic Ideal of Isaiah was the kingdom of God on earth. When the Messiah comes, the following conditions will exist:

1. Laws of God (Torah) will be recognized by all mankind; idolatry will be rejected.
2. Universal peace will prevail among all people.
3. There will be harmony between man and beast.

Apocalyptic Prophecies (Revelation):

4. Evil will be destroyed and good will triumph.
5. Exiles will return from all lands of the dispersion.
6. Jerusalem, the city of Zion and abode of God's glory in Isaiah's time, will be His habitation and the religious center of the world.
7. The dead will be resurrected: this is offered as a consolation for those whose suffering was not due to sinfulness.
8. Israel will rise from the lowest depths of degradation and suffering to the heights of respect and honor.

Famous Verses in Isaiah

1:2   Children I have reared and brought up
       And they have rebelled against Me.

1:3   The ox knows his owner,
       And the ass his master's crib;
       But Israel does not know,
       My people do not consider.

1:17   Learn to do well;
       Seek justice, relieve the oppressed,
       Judge the fatherless, plead for the widow.

1:18   If your sins be as scarlet,
Shall they be as white as snow?
If they are red like crimson,
Shall they be as wool?

2:1   It shall come to pass in the end of days
That the mountain of the Lord's house shall be
established as the top of the mountains,
And shall be exalted above the hills;
And all nations shall flow unto it.
[Almost identical to Micah 4:1.]

2:3   For out of Zion shall go forth the Law
And the word of God from Jerusalem.
[Identical to Micah 4:2.]

2:4   And they shall beat their swords into plowshares
And their spears into pruning hooks;
Nation shall not lift up sword against nation,
Neither shall they learn war any more.
[Found in Micah 4:3.]

11:6   And the wolf shall dwell with the lamb
And the leopard shall lie down with the kid;
And the calf and the young lion and the fatling
together;
And a little child shall lead them.

11:9   They shall not hurt nor destroy
In all My holy mountain
For the earth shall be full of the knowledge of
the Lord,
As the waters cover the sea.

12:2   Behold God is my salvation;
I will trust and will not be afraid;
For God the Lord is my strength and song
And He will be my salvation.
[This verse and the following are part of the
Havdalah service recited at the end of the Sab-
bath.]

12:3	With joy you shall draw water Out of the wells of salvation. [These are the words to a popular Israeli folk song and dance.]
22:13	"Let us eat and drink for tomorrow we shall die."
36:5–6	On whom do you trust? When you trust in Egypt, you depend on the staff of a weak reed. Whereon if a man lean, it will go into his hand and pierce it; So is Pharaoh king of Egypt to all who trust in him.
43:10	Before Me there was no God formed Neither shall there be any after Me.
43:11	I, I am the Lord. And beside Me there is no savior.
44:6	Thus said the Lord, the King of Israel And his Redeemer, the Lord of hosts I am the first and I am the last And beside Me there is no God.
45:5	I am the Lord and there is no other, Beside Me there is no other.
49:6	I will give you [make you] as a light for the nations.
59:20	A redeemer will come to Zion And to those in Jacob who turn away from transgression.
62:5	And as the bridegroom rejoices over the bride So shall your God rejoice over you. [Recited in the *Havdalah* service.]

JEREMIAH (PROPHETIC MISSION CIR. 625–585 B.C.E.)

Personal Background

Jeremiah's name means, "the Lord is exalted." The prophet came from a priestly family in Anatoth, which is about three miles from Jerusalem in the territory of Benjamin.

His prophetic mission lasted from 625 B.C.E. to after 586. His call came during Josiah's reign and continued until after the fall of Judah.

Of all the prophets, Jeremiah revealed the most about himself. He was humble and felt unequal to the task laid upon him. However, despite his modesty and self-doubts, he was bold and courageous. He spoke out fearlessly against the majority opinion and popular views. Jeremiah criticized the national policy of resisting Babylonia and seeking alliances with Egypt. He condemned the immorality and injustices of the kings, priests, nobility, and common people alike. He foretold the destruction of the state and exile of the people. He even questioned God and rebelled against his mission.

Jeremiah was a compassionate man. Even though he was put in stocks, imprisoned in a dungeon, and threatened with execution, he pitied the people and prayed to God for their welfare.

He had faith in God and in the ultimate restoration of Judah. As proof of his confidence in the return of Judah to its homeland and as a sign of encouragement to his fellow Judeans, he bought a plot of land during the siege of Jerusalem.

Religious and Social Conditions

The nation had ignored or forgotten the Law for the past seventy years, during the long reign of Menashe, his son, Amon, and the first ten years of Josiah's rule. In 621, the Book of Deuteronomy was discovered in the Temple. King Josiah instituted a religious reform, which did not last long after his death. People resumed the practice of idolatry. Adultery, deceit, and exploitation of the poor were rampant.

Jeremiah's Teachings

1. The one and only God rules *all* nature. Only He is to be worshipped. Idols are impotent.
2. God demands justice and righteousness. He will reward and punish according to man's behavior. Jeremiah's question of why the wicked prosper was not answered by God except through admonitions to have faith and patience.
3. The nation of Israel will be conquered and exiled for its faithlessness and sinfulness.
4. Through suffering the Jews will be purged of their sins.
5. God is omnipresent and omnipotent. Therefore, the exiles in Babylonia can seek and pray to Him there, also.
6. The Lord is God to all mankind. However, there is a special relationship (Covenant) between God and Israel. God has chosen Israel in consideration of Israel's acceptance of Him and His laws (Torah).
7. This Covenant does not free Jews from obedience to the laws, but rather imposes penalties for disobedience.

8. Despite punishment and national calamity, the Cove-
    nant between God and Israel remains. The land of
    Israel will always belong to the nation of Israel.
9. Even though the Temple and Jerusalem are sacred,
    they could, and would, be destroyed because of the
    evil of the people. Judeans thought both were invio-
    lable.
10. Like Isaiah, Jeremiah did not denounce sacrifice and
    ritual when performed with sincerity and accompa-
    nied by moral behavior. Condemnation came when
    these qualities were absent.

Message of Consolation

Jeremiah assured the Jews that despite the degradation
and loss of their land, they would return to it and rebuild
it. The nations that oppressed and fought against Israel
would be punished. He prophesied doom on Egypt,
Philistia, Moab, Ammon, Edom, Syria, and Babylonia.

Later Years of Jeremiah

Nebuchadnezzar, king of Babylonia, was friendly to
Jeremiah. He gave the prophet the choice of going into
exile or remaining in Judah. Jeremish chose the latter.
Nebuchadnezzar appointed Gedaliah governor over the
remnant of Judah. Many Jews who had fled to surrounding countries for refuge during the Babylonian assault
returned to Judah when they learned that a Jew had been
made governor over the land.

Ishmael, a Judean of royal blood, treacherously murdered Gedaliah and many Jews and Babylonians with
him. Ishmael's motive may have been resentment at
being passed over for governor. Jews feared to remain

in Judah despite Jeremiah's assurances and his warning against flight to Egypt which, he foretold, would be conquered by Babylonia. The people did not heed Jeremiah and migrated to Egypt, taking the prophet and Baruch, his friend and secretary, with them.

Famous Verses in Jeremiah

5:21	They have eyes and see not, They have ears and hear not.
8:22	Is there no balm in Gilead? Is there no physician there? Why then is there not *the healing of the daughter of my people?* [This is the motto of Hadassah.]
12:2	Why do the wicked prosper?
13:23	Can a Negro change his skin? Or a leopard his spots?
15:10	I have not lent, neither have men lent to me; Yet everyone curses me.
16:14–15	The time is coming when people shall . . . say . . . "As the Lord lives, who brought Israel back from the land of the north and from all the lands to which He banished them" that I will return them to their land which I gave to their forefathers.
22:13	Woe unto him who builds his house by unjust means And his upper rooms by fraud.
23:3	I will gather the remnant of My flock From all the lands where I scattered them And I will return them to their dwelling place And they shall be fruitful and multiply.

31:7	I will gather them from the remotest regions of the earth.
31:12	I will turn their mourning into joy And will comfort them and make them rejoice from their sorrow.
31:14	A voice is heard in Ramah, Lamentations and bitter weeping, Rachel weeping for her children; She refuses to be comforted for her children Because they are not [alive or in Israel].
31:28	The fathers have eaten sour grapes And the children's teeth are set on edge. [A similar phrase is found in Ezekiel 18:2.]
33:10	Again it shall be heard . . . In the cities of Judah and in the streets of Jerusalem
33:11	The voice of joy and the voice of gladness The voice of the bridegroom and the voice of the bride. [These words from 33:10 and 33:11 are written on the *ketubah* or marriage contract and recited during the marriage ceremony.] The voice of those who say, "Give thanks to the Lord of hosts For His mercy endures forever." [From the liturgy; also found in Psalms.]

EZEKIEL (PROPHETIC MISSION CIR. 592–572 B.C.E.)

Personal Background

Little is told about the prophet in his book, except that he came from a priestly family, that his wife died suddenly, and that he was exiled in 597 B.C.E., along with the king and the aristocracy. His prophetic mission lasted from 592 to 572. He died in Babylon, where a synagogue and a tomb commemorated him for centuries. His name means, "God will strengthen."

Characteristics of Ezekiel's Prophecy

Differences with Other Prophets

1. He was a prophet of the exile, the only one whose prophetic activity lay outside the land of Israel (in Babylonia).

2. He was the only one addressed as "son of man," which stressed that he was just a mortal even though he saw the Divine Glory.

3. His visions contain a strong element of mysticism, which provided messages of comfort:

The *Merkava* was a divine throne chariot, which departed because of the idolatry and corruption in the land. It later returned to Jerusalem. The chariot symbolized the presence of God. The vision was an assurance that God would be with Israel in exile and return the nation to its land.

The Vision of the dry bones symbolized Israel's regeneration. Finding himself in a valley of scattered, dry bones, the prophet saw them join together and form into bodies, which were then infused with the breath of life. Here, too, was the promise of the resurrection of the nation after defeat and captivity.

Gog was a symbolic figure of evil and danger whose attack on Israel was thwarted.

4. Ezekiel spoke or wrote mainly in prose, despite his use of symbolism and allegory.

5. Some of his descriptions of the Temple of the future and ritual in it were at variance with the Torah.

6. He preached individual responsibility and moral freedom. No one would be punished for the sins of his ancestors. Nor was behavior predetermined.

Similarities with Other Prophets

1. He performed symbolic acts:

He joined two sticks, which symbolized the unification of Judah and Israel.

He did not express bereavement over his wife's death, in accordance with God's command to him. This symbolized the shock that would overcome the Judeans already in Babylon when they learned of the fall of Jerusalem and the deaths of their dear ones who were left behind.

He was to prepare for exile by collecting articles for use on a journey and do it so that people would see him.

2. He used allegory:

He spoke of two adulterous sisters (Samaria and Judah) making alliances with Assyria and Babylonia.

He described two eagles, which represented Egypt and Babylonia.

He used a parable of a pot in which the meat put into it for cooking represented the people who would be caught in the Babylonian siege of Jerusalem. These people would be murdered or exiled until all of them would be lost.

He wrote of a crocodile captured and drawn by hooks, which symbolized Egypt and its fate.

3. He emphasized the need for people to return to the Torah.

4. He denounced Israel's sins and prophesied the fall of Jerusalem and the destruction of the state.

5. Ezekiel condemned and proclaimed the downfall of Israel's heathen neighbors.

6. He assured Israel that its enemies would receive their deserved punishment.

7. He expressed the messianic message that Israel and Judah would be united and restored to their land, that they would live in peace, and that God would be recognized by all peoples.

Contents of the Book

With the most methodical arrangement of all the Prophetic books, it contains forty-eight chapters, equally divided in two sections.

Chapters 1–24 tell of the siege and fall of Jerusalem and the destruction of Judah:

Revelation of the Merkava to Ezekiel and his appointment as Prophet.

Prophecies of destruction of the nation.

Condemnation of sinful practices of the people and their punishment.

Condemnation of false prophets giving false hope that Jerusalem was inviolable.

Censure of Zedekiah, the last king of Judah, who turned to Egypt for help against Babylonia.

Chapters 25–48 tell of the regeneration of Israel:

Annihilation of hostile, heathen neighbors who had gloated over Judah's fall and aided its enemies Ammon, Moab, Edom, Philistia, Phoenicia, Assyria, Egypt.

Restoration, redemption, and rebuilding of Judah and Israel.

Reunion of Judah and Israel.

Plan of the Temple of the future with a new order.

Redistribution of the land among the tribes, with the *Nasi*, or leader, of the people responsible for them and for religious observance.

Famous Verses in Ezekiel

12:2   Son of man, you dwell in the midst of the rebellious house that have eyes to see, and see not, that have ears to hear, and hear not.
[Similar to Jeremiah 5:21.]

18:20 The soul that sins, it shall die; the son shall not bear the iniquity of the father, and the father shall not bear the iniquity of the son; the righteousness of the righteous shall be upon him and the wickedness of the wicked shall be upon him.

33:11 Return, return from your evil ways.

37:21 I will take the children of Israel from among the nations, where they have gone, and will gather

them from everywhere and restore them to their
land.

37:25   They will live in the land that I gave to Jacob, My
servant, where your ancestors lived. They and their
descendants shall live there forever.

THE TWELVE (MINOR) PROPHETS
(CIR. 760–445 B.C.E.)

The so-called Minor Prophets are minor only in their brevity, not in their importance. In the Hebrew Bible these prophets are grouped together and are called "The Twelve." Their writings are brief enough to include in one volume because, in many cases, only fragments of their messages have survived. However, their teachings and preachings are nonetheless important and eloquent.

The Twelve Prophets and the approximate dates of their mission or, as in the case of Jonah, the date of composition, are as follows:

1. Hosea, 760–720 B.C.E.
2. Joel, before 800 or after 500
3. Amos, 765–750
4. Obadiah, 586
5. Jonah, fifth century
6. Micah, 739–687
7. Nahum, sometime between 663 and 608
8. Habakkuk, 600
9. Zephaniah, 637–607
10. Haggai, 520
11. Zechariah, 520–480
12. Malachi, 460–445

Hosea

Personal Background

Hosea came from the Northern Kingdom of Israel, where he prophesied. His mission lasted from 760 to 720 B.C.E., or until the fall of the Northern Kingdom and the exile of Israel by the Assyrians. He was partly contemporaneous with Isaiah, and his name roughly has the same meaning: "God saves."

Contents of the Book

The book is divided into two parts:

1. Hosea's personal life
2. Denunciation of all levels of society and warning of punishment awaiting them for sinfulness and infidelity to God

Hosea's life was an allegory for the relationship between God and Israel. He married Gomer, at God's command. She bore him a son and then became a harlot. She bore two more children, whose names symbolized God's attitude toward Israel in its infidelity to Him. The names are *Lo Ruhama,* meaning "no pity," and *Lo Ami*, "not My people."

Gomer's infidelity and Hosea's ransoming of her symbolized Israel's infidelity to God and His eventual redeeming of Israel after the nation had been purged of its sinfulness.

Hosea's impassioned addresses and teachings:

1. Condemned the priesthood for their greed.
2. Denounced the kings for leading the people into idolatry in order to lure them away from the Temple in Jerusalem and strengthen their own power.
3. Rejected sacrifices and worship without morality.
4. Opposed alliances with other countries because this introduced foreign religions and customs. These led to assimilation, loss of identity, and national disunity.

5. Warned of inevitable exile as punishment for immorality.
6. Especially cautioned against an alliance with Egypt.

After warning the nation of the dire fate awaiting them, Hosea, in true prophetic style, consoled them. God would again love and protect His people when they had been purified of their sins through the punishment of exile.

Famous Verses in Hosea

6:6   For I desire mercy and not sacrifice
      And the knowledge of God rather than burnt offerings.
7:8   Ephraim is half-baked.
      [Literally, a cake not turned.]
10:12 Sow according to righteousness
      Reap according to mercy.
10:13 You have plowed wickedness, you have reaped iniquity.
13:2 They that sacrifice men kiss calves.

Joel

Personal Background

Little is known about this prophet except that he lived in Jerusalem and may have been a priest. The book gives no clear indication when he lived. Speculation ranges from before 800 to after 500 B.C.E. Those who accept the former date do so because the book fails to mention Assyria, which did not emerge as a power until about 760. Others consider Joel's description of a plague of locusts as an allegorical allusion to the Assyrian invasion. This would place him in the mid- to late eighth century, contemporary with Hosea and Amos. This is the traditional view and the reason for the book's placement between these two Prophets. Some scholars consider the book postexilic and date it to the mid-fifth century.

The name Joel means, "the Lord is God."

Contents of the Book

The book has four chapters. The account starts with a plague of locusts, which devastate the land. This may be a real occurrence or represent the Assyrian invasion. The description of the effect of such a plague on life and economy is vivid and scientifically accurate.

The people are exhorted to be righteous. Then God will restore their land to peace and prosperity and imbue the entire nation with the spirit of prophecy.

The last chapter depicts Judgment Day, on which God will punish Egypt, Edom, Philistia, and Phoenicia for their cruelty to Israel. The prophet promises that Israel's enemies will be as desolate as Israel will be prosperous.

Famous Verse in Joel

4:2   I will gather all the nations together . . .
       And will bring them to judgment
       For My people and My heritage, Israel.

Amos

Personal Background

Amos came from the mountaintop village of Tekoa in Judah but prophesied in Israel. His mission lasted from 765 to 750 B.C.E., making him possibly the earliest of the Twelve Prophets. He worked as a herdsman and also dressed or tended sycamore trees. As such, he was a simple man of humble background, used to an austere life. Despite his distance from Samaria, he was well aware of the social, political, and religious conditions there. He was offended by the luxurious life and the immorality of the Israelites and became a social reformer.

Contents of the Book

Amos denounced the neighboring nations of Israel and Judah for their brutality and constant attacks. He warned of the destruction of Syria, Phoenicia, Edom, Ammon, and Moab.

He then indicted Judah and Israel for their sins of idolatry, exploitation of the poor, and corruption. He concentrated his condemnation on Israel, asserting that its sinfulness and immorality would lead to exile. He warned that Israel was not immune to punishment because God had previously favored her, but would be judged more severely for not appreciating His benevolence.

Amos particularly condemned the luxurious life of the aristocracy and the extravagance of the women, which led to exploitation and enslavement of the poor. He censured the hypocrisy of observing religious rituals and then engaging in fraudulent behavior.

He called on Israel to repent in order to avoid Assyrian exile. His five visions foretold the doom that would befall the nation. He used symbols such as a plague of locusts, a fire, a tottering wall, a basket of late, ripe fruit, and ruins of a shrine to denote Israel's inevitable destruction.

Amos offered a final message of hope that Israel would eventually return from captivity, be united again with Judah, and be led by a descendant of David. He envisioned a prosperous land in which the people would live in peace.

Famous Verses in Amos

1:3   For three transgressions of Damascus
Yea, for four, I will not reverse it [punishment].
[These words were the title and lyrics in a popular song during the Six Day War in Israel in 1967.]

2:6   Because they sell the righteous for silver
And the needy for a pair of shoes.

4:1   Hear this you cows of Bashan
That are in the mountain of Samaria
Who oppress the poor, who crush the needy
Who say unto their husbands, "Bring that we may feast."

5:24 Let justice well up as waters
And righteousness as a mighty stream.

Obadiah

Background

Nothing is mentioned about the prophet's personal life. His name means "servant (or worshipper) of God." He probably lived in 586 B.C.E. and witnessed the destruction of the Temple. This is the shortest book in the Bible, consisting of one chapter with twenty-one verses. Its single theme is an imprecation on Edom.

The book conveys the following messages:

1. The denunciation of Edom.
2. The cry of oppressed Jews throughout the centuries for vengeance against their enemies and hope of their own eventual triumph.
3. Prophecy of Edom's downfall and demise for its cruelty and perfidy during Jerusalem's agony.
4. Edom became a stock term for cruel and treacherous enemies of the Jews. For example, the Romans were cryptically referred to as Edom.

Historical Background

Edom was related to Judah through his descent from Esau, Jacob's brother. The Edomites not only refused to help their brethren during the Babylonian destruction of Jerusalem, they despoiled them and cut off their escape. Obadiah's prediction of Edom's destruction and demise were realized. The Nabateans conquered their land and Edom disappeared as a nation in the first century of the Common Era.

Jonah

General Information

Scholars believe that the name of an eighth-century Prophet, mentioned briefly in 2 Kings, was given to the book and that the anonymous author lived in the fifth century. Unlike other Prophetic books, this one contains primarily, and almost exclusively, the author's experiences, but not his utterances. No historical or archaeological evidence has been found for this story.

Narrative

Jonah was sent by God to announce to Nineveh in Assyria its imminent destruction. Jonah tried to evade his duty and fled. He took a ship from Jaffa to Tarshish (Spain). A storm came up at sea which threatened to cause the drowning of all on board. The sailors prayed to their gods and then cast lots to determine who on the ship was the cause of the tempest. The lot fell on Jonah, and he admitted his culpability. He was cast into the sea at his own request and immediately, the storm ceased.

Jonah was swallowed by a great fish and thus saved from drowning. He thanked God. After three days, he was ejected on dry land. He received a second command from God, which he obeyed immediately. He came to Nineveh and pronounced that doom would befall the city within forty days. The Ninevites, from the king on down, accepted the warning. They repented by fasting and making reparations for their past sins and were forgiven.

Jonah had known this might happen. The Assyrians had been cruel enemies of Israel, and he did not want to help them. He was angry about the outcome. He took up abode outside the city and was sheltered from the sun by a fast-growing plant. When the plant withered and Jonah was exposed to the sun and hot wind, he became angry about the destruction of the plant.

The lesson God drew for Jonah was that while the prophet regretted the loss of a plant for which he did not labor, how much more did God pity 120,000 Ninevites who were His creatures.

Teachings of the Book

The book can be understood as an allegory or a parable.

ALLEGORY

Jonah is Israel; his symbolic name means dove
His disappearance into the sea is exile
His ejection on dry land is Israel's restoration

PARABLE (TO TEACH LESSONS)

God accepts repentance
Gentiles are also God's creatures
[Jonah knew both these concepts]
It is wrong to begrudge to the Gentiles God's love and
   forgiveness

The book is read on the Day of Atonement because repentance and forgiveness are so much a part of the story, as they are of the holiday.

Micah

Personal Background

The prophet's name means, "who is like the Lord." Micah came from Moreshet-Gat, near the Philistine border in Judah. He prophesied mostly in Judah, but partly in Israel. His mission lasted from 739 to 687, during the reigns of Yotam, Ahaz, and Hezekiah (almost identical with Isaiah). There are verses in the books of the two prophets that are almost identical. This means that one could have quoted from the other or that they both had a common source.

Micah was courageous and fearless in his denunciation of the rich and powerful in Judean society. He had a deep sympathy for the underdog, the poor, and the victims of social injustice. Despite his condemnation, he had a love for all Israel and pitied them their inevitable fate.

Historical Background

During the eighth century, Israel and Judah were prosperous and engaged in the pursuit of commerce and wealth. Jereboam II of Israel and Uzziah (Azariah) of Judah had long, successful reigns during which they extended the borders of their kingdoms and enabled the latter to develop trade.

Along with the wealth came greed and unscrupulous competition. The rich enlarged their estates and eventually dispossessed the peasants. The latter had no redress and went to live in the cities to seek a livelihood. The cities reflected the extremes of wealth and poverty, becoming centers of both splendor and squalor. The nation was divided into classes: the landed and the expropriated.

There was neither charity nor justice for the poor and weak in society. Commerce brought an exchange of ideas, religious cults, and standards of luxury that were foreign to Hebrew agricultural society, which was based on laws of the Torah and land tenure.

Messages of the Book

As in most prophetic books, there is a threefold message of denunciation, warning, and comfort, namely:

1. Denunciation of social evils such as exploitation and expropriation of the poor; condemnation of priests, false prophets, corrupt judges, and leaders who made oppression possible.
2. Warning that corruption and evil would lead to the destruction of Jerusalem, the defeat of Israel and Judah, and exile.
3. Comfort and reassurance of the return from exile and eventual restoration of a united Judah and Israel.

In addition, Micah stressed other ideas:

He spoke of a Messianic Age heralded by a descendant of David who would rule from Jerusalem.

His description of the Messianic Age included universal peace, worldwide righteousness and justice, and the recognition of Israel's God as the one, true God and His Law as supreme throughout the earth.

Micah did *not* speak about idolatry and political movements; he was concerned about expunging social injustice.

Famous Verses in Micah

4:1   In the end of days it shall come to pass
That the mountain of the Lord's house shall be established as the top of the mountains,
And it shall be exalted above the hills;
And nations shall flow unto it.

4:2   For out of Zion shall go forth the law
      And the word of the Lord from Jerusalem.

4:3   And they shall beat their swords into plowshares,
      And their spears into pruning hooks;
      Nation shall not lift up sword against nation,
      Neither shall they learn war any more.

4:4   But they shall sit every man under his vine and under
      his fig tree;
      And none shall make them afraid.
      [Micah 4:1, 2, 3, 4 is almost identical with Isaiah 2:2, 3,
      4.]

6:8   It has been told you, O man, what is good,
      And what the Lord requires of you:
      Only to do justice, and love mercy, and walk humbly
      with your God.

7:7   As for me, I will look to the Lord;
      I will wait for the God of my salvation;
      My God will hear me.

Nahum

Personal Background

Nahum lived in Judah during the reigns of Amon and
Josiah. Nothing is known of his personal life. His prophecy is set any time between 663 and 608, during the
period of Assyrian domination of Judah. His name conveys the meaning of comfort or consolation.

Historical Background

Assyria was a dominant power whose yoke lay heavily
on Judah. Its rulers were notorious for their ruthless-

ness and brutality. Nineveh, the capital, was a center of commerce and a repository of wealth taken from conquered nations. Nineveh and the Assyrian Empire fell in 612 to Babylonia, to the relief and joy of its many victim nations. This empire, people, and culture completely disappeared, as stated in Nahum's prophecy.

Josiah's reign lasted from 637 to 607. In 621 the Book of Deuteronomy was discovered in the Temple. Josiah instituted a religious reform in Judah. He lost his life in battle against Assyria at Megiddo.

Contents of the Book

The book contains only three chapters. Nahum gave a graphic, though visionary, account of the fall of Nineveh, which includes invasion, flight of its inhabitants, destruction of the city, and the enormous spoils left for the victors. The prophet foresaw a messenger announcing the good news of Nineveh's downfall, as well as the annihilation of all who oppressed Israel and opposed God.

The focus of Nahum's preaching was that God would bring judgment on all evil nations and deliver His people, Israel.

Habakkuk

Personal Background

Little is known of his personal life. He was a Levite and prophesied in Judah sometime between 607 and 586. The date of this prophecy is most likely 600. This was after the defeat of Assyria and the ascendance of Babylonia.

It is believed that Habakkuk escaped to Egypt during the fall of Jerusalem in 586 and returned after the exiles went into captivity. By then, most of the Babylonians had left. His name conveys the meaning of "embrace" or "caress."

Contents of the Book

The book contains only three chapters. The prophet challenged God for allowing the wicked to prosper and the innocent to suffer. He complained that God did nothing to stop injustice and oppression. (Jeremiah, Job, and Malachi also wrestled with this problem.) God's reply to Habakkuk was that the Chaldeans (Babylonians) were his means for punishing Israel for its wrongdoings. Habakkuk was shocked that God would allow a nation that was more guilty and far more evil to be His tool to destroy Israel.

God's answer to this dilemma was that the righteous would live by their faithfulness. The meaning of this phrase is that the Israelites who were loyal to moral precepts might suffer for a time but would eventually be vindicated, while the wicked would enjoy only temporary success and in the end be destroyed.

The prophet foretold that Israel would survive to taunt its oppressor (Babylonia) and that this would be a lesson for the world to see. Habakkuk described, in vivid, anthropomorphic imagery, God's overthrow of the enemy.

Unlike most of the other prophets, Habakkuk directed his attack on the sins of the oppressor nations, contrasted with which, Israel's backslidings paled into insignificance.

Famous Verses in Habakkuk

1:2   How long, O Lord, shall I cry,
      And You will not hear?
      I cry out unto You of violence
      And You will not save.

2:4   The righteous shall live by his faithfulness.

2:9   Woe to him who seeks ill-gotten gains for his
      house.

2:14 For the earth shall be filled
      With the knowledge of the glory of the Lord,
      As the waters cover the earth.
      [This is similar to the last two lines of Isaiah 11:9.]

2:20 The Lord is in His holy temple;
      Let all the earth keep silent before Him.
      [These are opening words in many church services.]

Zephaniah

Personal Background

Zephaniah was an aristocrat of royal descent who lived
and prophesied in Judah during the early period of
Josiah's reign, while the latter was still in his minority.
This places Zephaniah before Nahum and Habakkuk and
makes him a contemporary of Jeremiah. It is believed
that he had an influence on young Josiah and the religious reformation which the king instituted.

The prophet saw at firsthand the demoralization
among the privileged classes who aped foreign customs
and practiced idolatry.

His name means, "he whom God has hidden" and
seems to have no connection with his prophecy.

Contents of the Book

The three chapters of this book are fragments of the prophet's writings, which include the following messages:

1. Zephaniah expressed the usual prophetic themes of the punishment of the wicked, vindication of the faithful, and promise of their salvation.
2. The prophet was a fervent nationalist and denounced assimilation. He condemned the pursuit of wealth at the cost of the Jewish heritage of social justice.
3. Zephaniah did not champion the cause of the poor and oppressed as such, but declared that salvation would spring from the poor and humble. He denounced the idolatry and injustice of the nobility and rulers.
4. He was concerned with the downfall of Judah and the salvation of the remnant of Israel.
5. God's judgment would fall on the enemies of Israel: Philistia, Moab, Ammon, Egypt, and Assyria.
6. The main burden of his prophecy was that a universal Day of Judgment would bring salvation to the righteous and faithful in Israel and punishment to those who perverted justice.

Famous Verses in Zephaniah

1:13 They will build houses, but shall not inhabit them, They will plant vineyards, but shall not drink the wine thereof.
[Similar thoughts are expressed in Amos 5:11 and Micah 6:15.]

3:14 Sing, O daughter of Zion,

Shout O Israel;
Be glad and rejoice with all your heart
O daughter of Jerusalem.

3:15   The Lord has taken away your judgments [punishment]
He has cast out your enemy;
The King of Israel, the Lord, is in your midst
You shall not fear evil any more.

Postexilic Prophets: Haggai, Zechariah, and Malachi

These three prophets dealt with the restoration of the Second Temple. The Talmud states that they were the founders of the Great Synagogue or Great Assembly, the supreme council during the Second Temple period.

Historical Background (538–516 B.C.E.)

538   Cyrus issued a decree that Jews could return to Judea and rebuild the Temple.

537   About 50,000 Jews set out for Judea under the joint leadership of Zerubabel, a civil leader and descendant of David, and Joshua, a religious leader and High Priest. The former was appointed governor of the repatriates by the Persian authorities.

536   The foundations of the Temple were laid. The Samaritans (foreign colonists settled in Samaria by the Assyrians almost two centuries earlier) sabotaged the Jews. By intrigues and misrepresentations to the Persian authorities, they brought the work to a halt. Conditions worsened with a combination of attacks on Jews by Samaritans and drought, which caused poverty and famine.

520   Darius came to the throne and followed the same liberal policy as Cyrus, which was to allow freedom

of religious worship to conquered peoples. He gave permission for the resumption of work on the Temple, which had already begun under the inspiration of Haggai. Haggai, an old but vigorous man, came to Jerusalem to encourage the Jews to continue rebuilding the Temple. Zechariah came to Jerusalem shortly after Haggai. Under his moving spirit, the goal was accomplished.

516   The completion and dedication of the Temple were due largely to the inspiration and encouragement of Haggai and Zechariah. This occurred exactly seventy years after the destruction of the First Temple, as prophesied by Jeremiah.

The Talmud declares that with the death of Haggai, Zechariah, and Malachi, prophecy departed from Israel.

Haggai

Personal Background

Nothing is known about his personal life. Haggai must have remembered the First Temple and was, therefore, very old at the time of his mission to Jerusalem in 520 B.C.E. Most of his life was spent in Babylonia.

Contents of the Book

The book has only two chapters, containing four short addresses to the Jews in Jerusalem. Haggai gave hope and encouragement to the struggling community, which had returned from captivity.

He inspired the people to resume building the Temple by telling them:

1. Their misfortunes were due to neglect of their holy work.
2. By rebuilding the Temple, they would see God's return to them and greater prosperity.
3. This Temple would be more glorious than the first. Since the early structure of the Second Temple was very modest by comparison with the First Temple, this was a hope for future elegance, which was accomplished by Herod.

Famous Verse in Haggai

1:6 You have sown much and brought in little,
     You eat, but are not sated,
     You drink, but are not satisfied,
     You dress, but have no warmth,
     And he who earns wages, earns them
     For a bag with holes.

Zechariah

Personal Background

Zechariah was both a priest and prophet. His mission began in 520 B.C.E. as a younger contemporary of Haggai and continued until about 480. His name means, "remembrance of God" and may allude to verses in this book that testify to God's remembrance of Judah and its restoration.

Contents of the Book

The book is divided into two parts: chapters 1 through 8 deal with the prophet's messages and preaching; chapters 9 through 14 deal with assurances of the future.

Part 1

Zechariah wanted the restoration of the Temple, but he was not a religious formalist. He preached a spiritual religion in the tradition of Hosea, Amos, Micah, Isaiah, and Jeremiah. His prophecies were characterized by visions with angels illustrating his messages and interpreting his visions.

His preaching contained these messages:

1. Justice and mercy were required of people, and ritual was no substitute for righteousness.
2. Messianism, which is the establishment of the Kingdom of God on earth, would be effected by a king-messiah, who would rule according to God's laws. In the Messianic Age, there will be world peace and no sin.

Part 2

Some scholars doubt that Zechariah wrote this section because many of the features of the first eight chapters are absent here. There are no visions or angels, and neither the prophet nor his contemporaries are mentioned. There is no allusion to the building of the Temple. Moreover, the Persian period is not mentioned. Instead, a very different chapter of history is described in which Greece figured prominently.

Others, however, see the last six chapters as the work of Zechariah at a different time of his life and a different period of history. There is a similar feeling of hope and expectation in both sections regarding the restoration of Jerusalem and the centrality of the Temple in the nation's religious life. There are strong messianic

hopes for peace and prosperity, and the expectation of
God's providence extending over the whole world.

Zechariah was a young man when he began his mission in Jerusalem. His main concern then was the rebuilding of the Temple. He could have easily lived
through the period in which Persia came into conflict
with Greece and lost the naval battle at Salamis in 480.
He anticipated the demise of Persia and the rise of
Greece.

Israel was living securely under Persian rule. Zechariah
recognized the threat of Greece to Israel's political security and the danger of Hellenism to Jewish religious
values and philosophy. Within the context of this insight and anticipation, Zechariah assured Israel of God's
continued protection and inspired the nation with hope
for the future. Zechariah prophesied that the Greeks
would be defeated by the Jews, which some later saw
as a prediction of the Maccabean victory over the Syrian Greeks.

The different conditions in the world in the forty years
between the first and second parts of the book would
account for differences in scenery, subjects, and concerns.

Famous Verses in Zechariah

  4:6   Not by might, nor by power, but by My spirit [will
        the Temple be restored] said the Lord of hosts.
  8:3   Thus said the Lord: I have returned to Zion and
        will dwell in the midst of Jerusalem; and Jerusa-
        lem shall be called the city of truth and the moun-
        tain of the Lord of hosts, the holy mountain.
  8:8   I will bring them [Israel] and they shall dwell in the
        midst of Jerusalem; and they shall be My people

and I will be their God in truth and in righteousness.

14:9   The Lord shall be King over all the earth.
In that day shall the Lord be One and His name
one.

Malachi

Personal Background

The author is anonymous. His name means, "My messenger," which describes the prophet's mission. He min-
istered in Jerusalem during the Persian period, after the
Temple had been rebuilt. The time is after Zerubabel
(538–516 B.C.E.) and before Nehemiah (445–424); in other
words, sometime between 500 and 460 or 460 and 445.

Historical Background

Conditions in Jerusalem at the time of Malachi's mission were similar to those which existed during the time
of Nehemiah (445) and Ezra (380):

1. The Temple service was not observed.
2. Priests were remiss in their duties.
3. People were indifferent to, or sceptical of, religion.
4. Men divorced their Jewish wives and intermarried.
5. Morals were lax.

Messages of the book were delivered in dialectical
(question-and-answer) style.
   1. God still loves Israel, but the nation must merit His
love.

2. The people must restore the Temple ritual and meet their religious obligations as a show of faith and love of God.

3. Not only ritual, but ethical behavior as well, must be observed:

> Malachi denounced adultery, perjury, and the oppression of widows and orphans.
>
> He condemned the divorce of Jewish wives and marriage with Gentiles as disloyalty to God and the nation.

4. Sincere heathen worship is an offering to God; this is a concept of universalism, later developed in Judaism.

5. The Day of the Lord, Judgment Day, will come and on it:

> Israel will be judged, not the other nations.
> The wicked will be destroyed and the righteous rewarded.
> Elijah's coming will precede and foretell this event.
> The Messianic Era will follow Judgment Day and bring peace and harmony to the world.

6. As the last of the prophets, Malachi preached strict observance of the Torah.

Famous Verses in Malachi

1:6   A son honors his father, and a servant his master
      If I am a father, where is My honor?
      And if I am a master, where is My fear?
2:10 Have we not all one father?
      Has not one God created us?

Why do we betray, every man his brother,
Profaning the covenant of our fathers?

3:1   Behold, I am sending My messenger
And he will clear the way before Me.

3:23   Behold, I will send you Elijah the prophet
Before the coming
Of the great and terrible day of the Lord.

4

HOLY WRITINGS (*KETUVIM*): HISTORICAL BOOKS

The Hagiographa comprises books of liturgical poetry, secular poetry, wisdom literature, and historical works.

In this division of Bible books I do not follow the canonical order as I do in the Torah and prophetic sections. Instead, I first review and summarize the *historical books and in their historical order*, thus continuing the sequence of Jewish history that started with Genesis. The historical books in this section are: Daniel, Esther, Nehemiah, Ezra, and 1 and 2 Chronicles. The latter two books, the last in the Jewish canon, provide a summary of historical events and genealogies from Adam to Cyrus, recounting events and material covered in previous books.

In order to acquire a proper historical perspective of where each famous person, event, or book fits, the reader will find it useful to refer to the chapter of important dates in Jewish history at the beginning of the book.

After summarizing the historical books, I review the collection of Wisdom Literature, which includes Proverbs, Ecclesiastes, and Job.

Finally, I review those books in the "Scrolls" that are not included in the historical section (Esther) or Wisdom Literature (Ecclesiastes) of the Hagiographa. Altogether, there are five books referred to as Scrolls. Each of them is read on a different Jewish holiday. Song of Songs is read at Passover. Ruth is read on the holiday of Shavuot (Feast of Weeks). Lamentations is read on the mourning day of the Ninth of Av. Ecclesiastes is read on Succot (Feast of Tabernacles). Esther is read on Purim.

It is interesting to note that of the Five Scrolls, the central character in three is a heroine. Ruth and Esther, besides being the heroines of their books, are also eponymous. The Shulamite girl is clearly the sole heroic figure in Song of Songs. The other two Scrolls do not mention individuals. Lamentations is a dirge, and Ecclesiastes is a philosophical work.

Although these latter five books are referred to as Scrolls, the reader should be aware that indeed, all the Bible books were written on scrolls. The Five Books of Moses are found (today) in one enormous scroll in which the numerous segments are glued together.

The last book condensed in this compendium is the Book of Psalms.

DANIEL

Personal Background

Daniel came from an aristocratic family. In 597 B.C.E. at about age fourteen, he was exiled to Babylonia in the first captivity, which included the aristocracy and skilled artisans. Daniel was educated at Nebuchadnezzar's court with other promising boys. He proved to be brilliant and staunchly faithful to his religion.

Daniel's wisdom brought him fame and responsibility in a long career under the Babylonian kings Nebuchadnezzar and Belshazzar, under Darius the Mede, and under the Persian king, Cyrus. Daniel's interpretation of dreams and visions played a significant role in his fame and success.

He lived to see the return of the Jews to Judah in 538. According to tradition, he gave his office to Zerubabel and retired to Susa (Shushan) in Persia.

Daniel had great integrity and courage in the face of physical danger and threats to his position. He refused to eat nonkosher meat at the king's court. He prayed to God against the king's edict. Moreover, he related to Nebuchadnezzar the ominous portent of the king's dream.

His name means, "God is my judge."

Contents of the Book

The book is composed in two languages: Hebrew and Aramaic. It has twelve chapters and is divided into two equal sections of six chapters each. However, the chapters are not coincident with the two languages. The book was written on scrolls, some of which were in Hebrew and others in the vernacular, Aramaic. At the time of canonization, the documents were reproduced as they were found.

Chapters 1 through 6 relate six narratives of Daniel and his three companions, who were given Babylonian names as follows:

Daniel was called Belteshazzar
Hananiah was called Shadrach
Mishael was called Meshach
Azariah was called Abed-nego

The chapters related the following stories.

1. The four boys demonstrated their religious steadfastness at court by declining to eat the meat and drink the wine given them and insisting on other foods. They prospered and were promoted.

2. Daniel revealed and interpreted Nebuchadnezzar's dream of a colossal image of gold, silver, brass, and iron, which represented four kingdoms. These kingdoms are thought to represent either Babylonia, Media, Persia, and Greece or Babylonia, Persia, Greece, and Rome.

3. Daniel's three companions were thrown into a fiery furnace for not worshiping a ninety-foot golden image, yet they survived.

4. Daniel interpreted another dream of Nebuchadnezzar in which the king was likened to a felled tree and was told that he would go mad. After the fulfillment of the dream, the king repented of his sins.

5. Daniel told the portent of a message written on the wall of the palace during Belshazzar's reign which presaged his loss of the kingdom.

6. Daniel was cast into a lion's den for praying to his God. He was saved and subsequently elevated to eminence.

Chapters 7 through 12 describe four visions of Daniel.

7. Four animals represent four kingdoms: Babylonia, Media, Persia, and Greece.

8. There is a contest between two ferocious animals: a ram with two horns (Persia and Media) is destroyed by a goat (Greece), which is in turn crushed.

9. Daniel prayed for the redemption of Israel and received an explanation from the angel Gabriel of Jeremiah's prophecy of the seventy years between the destruction of the First Temple and the building of the Second. There is a cryptic reference to the period of the Second Temple.

10–12. Daniel fasted and prayed to receive a divine revelation about the future. An angel revealed the succession of kingdoms culminating in the death of a cruel, godless despot. There is a prediction of the triumph of righteousness. It is believed this will occur in the Messianic Era in the remote future, at which time the dead will be resurrected. Daniel did not understand the cryptic messages.

Characteristics of the Book

1. Daniel is not recognized in Jewish tradition as a prophet. His book is, therefore, included in the third division of the Hebrew Bible.
2. Some scholars place the composition of the book to the period of Ezra in Jerusalem (circa 400–380). Others date it to the second century B.C.E.
3. The book is apocalyptic, meaning that it speaks of the

distant future, as distinct from prophetic, which refers to the present and near future.

4. This is the only book in which angels have specific names. Two are mentioned, Michael and Gabriel. The former is regarded as the guardian angel of Israel.

5. The book conveys a belief in the immortality of the soul and resurrection of the dead. The former is implied in other books of the Hebrew Bible and the latter is found in Ezekiel.

Famous Verse in Daniel

5:25–28   *Mene Mene, Tekel Upharsin** This is the interpretation of the thing:
Mene—God has numbered your kingdom and brought it to an end.
Tekel—You are weighed in the balances and found wanting.
Peres*—Your kingdom is divided and given to the Medes and Persians.

Cyrus's decree permitting the return of the Jews to Judea and the rebuilding of the Temple occurred after the events recorded in Daniel and before the episodes referred to in the subsequent books in this section, namely, Esther, Nehemiah, Ezra, and 1 and 2 Chronicles.

The return to Zion occurred in at least a few stages. The first exiles returned with Zerubabel and Jeshua in 537. It can be assumed that Judeans continued coming back for the next twenty years, with the encouragement of the prophets Haggai and Zechariah. Nehemiah led

---

*The relation between these two words, *Upharsin* and *Peres*, can be seen in Hebrew; they have the same root.

the return of exiles about 445, and Ezra led returnees about 395.

Map 4-1 shows the approximate routes the exiles took from Persia and Babylonia to Judea.

Map 4-1 THE RETURN TO ZION (537-395 B.C.E.)

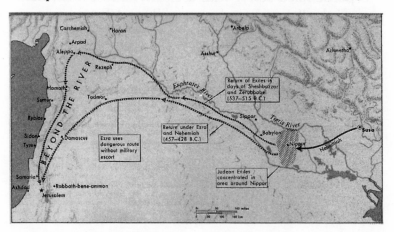

ESTHER

Characteristics of the Book

Esther is perhaps the most popular and best-known book of the Hebrew Bible. It has an exciting, dramatic, suspense-filled story, with a clearly drawn hero, heroine, and villain, plus a happy ending. All this is accomplished in ten short chapters.

Until the advent of Adolf Hitler, Haman was the prototype for the many persecutors of the Jews, and his plot was a standard for schemes against Jews. His downfall represented hope and triumph for persecuted Jews.

The author of the Book of Esther was either Mordecai, a member of the Great Synagogue, or some other member of that institution, or another person with intimate knowledge of the Persian court. There are numerous commentaries in Jewish literature on this book. The Apocrypha contains a "sequel" to Esther, called *Additions to the Book of Esther*.

This is the only book in the Bible in which the name of God and reference to Him are absent. It is also the only one in the Hebrew Bible not found among the Dead Sea Scrolls.

The names of four months in the Hebrew calendar are mentioned in the book of Esther: Tevet, Adar, Nissan, and Sivan. They were adopted by the Jews in Babylonia and are still in use today.

Historical Background

Persia, which included Media, was the dominant power for 200 years, from 538 to 332. The Persian Empire extended from India to Ethiopia.

Ahasueros (known in Greek as Xerxes I) reigned from 485 to 465. He was an extravagant, foolish, capricious king, as portrayed in Esther and by the Greek historian Herodotus. He engaged in two battles with Greece in 480. At Thermopylae, Ahasueros defeated the Spartan army, and at Salamis, the Athenians defeated the Persians in a crucial sea battle.

The Persian Empire had three capitals:

Susa (Shushan) in Persia
Ecbatana in Media
Babylon in Babylonia

The book revealed certain psychological insights into Jew-hatred. For example, it shows how a real or imagined personal grievance against one Jew has often become an excuse to attack the entire people. Moreover, an accusation that "Jews are different" because they observe a different religion and follow different customs has often been used as a justification for branding them disloyal to the country. Both these ploys were used by Haman and his spiritual successors.

Contents of the Book

At a large feast in Susa, amidst the revelry, King Ahasueros requested Queen Vashti "to show her beauty," which *may* have meant to appear nude. She refused and, upon the urging of his advisors, the king deposed her. He later regretted his action and sought another queen. A beauty contest was held throughout the empire. Esther, the niece of Mordecai the Jew, was selected as the new queen. She did not reveal her background, upon her uncle's advice.

Mordecai saved Ahasueros's life by informing him of a plot against him by his servants.

Haman the Agagite (a descendant of Agag the Amalekite, the leader of the traditional biblical enemy of Israel) was elevated to the post of grand vizier. When Mordecai would not bow down to him, Haman planned to exterminate all the Jews. He told the king of his plan to murder the Jews and appropriate their possessions for the Crown. Mordecai urged Esther to go to the king and plead the case of the Jews.

Meanwhile, Ahasueros was reminded of Mordecai's service to him, which he wished to reward. The king unwittingly appointed Haman to honor his enemy.

Esther invited the king to a banquet and presented her petition to him. Haman's downfall and execution followed, and Mordecai became prime minister. The king's decree could not be revoked, but a counterdecree was issued providing for the Jews to defend themselves and kill their attackers. They did so, and many of their enemies were killed. The book stresses that the Jews took no spoil or loot.

Mordecai instituted the holiday of Purim as an annual celebration. The Hebrew word means "lots." This refers to the lots that Haman cast to determine on which day he would order the murder of Jews.

Customs of the Holiday of Purim

1. Jews living in unwalled cities celebrate Purim on the 14th of Adar; Jews living in walled cities celebrate Purim on the 15th of Adar (in February or March). In Jerusalem, which is a walled city, residents have developed the custom of celebrating both days.

2. Jews read the Scroll of Esther in synagogues on the evening of Purim and the next morning. Women are obliged to attend that service, since it was a woman who saved the Jews.

3. Gifts are sent on Purim (usually of food), which are called *shalach manot*.

4. Celebrations include masquerades, carnivals, merrymaking, feasting, and drinking. The celebration of Mardi Gras is reminiscent of this aspect of Purim festivities, and it occurs at the same time of year as the Jewish holiday.

5. Special cakes are eaten, which are called in German *hamantashen* ("Haman's pockets"), and in Hebrew, *oznay haman* ("Haman's ears").

Famous Verses in Esther

4:13 Mordecai's message to Esther: Don't think that you will escape in the king's house the fate of all [your fellow] Jews.

4:14 For if you remain silent at this time, relief and deliverance will come from another place, but you and all your family will perish; and who knows, but you achieved royal estate for such a time as this.

8:16 The Jews had light and gladness, and joy and honor.

[This verse is included in the *Havdalah* service, with the addition of the words, "So be it with us."]

NEHEMIAH

Authorship and Date

Jewish tradition assigns the authorship of both Nehemiah and Ezra to the latter man. This very belief adds strength to the argument that Nehemiah *preceded* Ezra if the latter wrote both books, which are about the work of both men. There are many reasons for placing Nehemiah before Ezra, despite their inverted places in the canon. The dating here assumes the following:

Nehemiah lived during the reign of Artaxerxes I (465–424 B.C.E.). The events in his book cover the period 445–432. The book is about, but not by, Nehemiah.

Ezra lived during the reign of Artaxerxes II (404–358). His mission in Jerusalem lasted approximately from 397 to 380.

Personal Background

Nehemiah was a powerful personality who made a lasting impression on his generation and those following him. He was a vigorous, able, strong-willed leader. The religious practices and reforms that he instituted are observed to this day. His name means, "consolation of God."

Historical Background

Conditions in Judea were demoralized:

Intermarriage was rife.
Sabbath observance was ignored.
The Temple was neglected.

The poor were exploited by the rich.
There was no unity among the returned exiles.

The security of Jerusalem was endangered:

Jerusalem had no walls around it.
Samaritans attacked, sabotaged, and slandered Jews.[1]

Contents of the Book

Introduction

The book relates Nehemiah's life and work from the time he obtained permission of the Persian king to go to Judea to the occasion of his second visit to Jerusalem. In 445, Nehemiah received disturbing news of conditions in Judea. He prayed for, and was granted, permission to visit Jerusalem; he was appointed governor of Judea and was even given a military escort.

Work of Construction

Upon his arrival in Jerusalem in 444, Nehemiah inspected the city walls at night to determine their relative safety

---

1. The Samaritans were foreign colonists from Babylon and elsewhere who were settled in Samaria by Sargon in 721, after the fall of the Northern Kingdom and the exile of the Israelites. The Samaritans were a mixture of peoples and might have included some Israelites who had escaped exile. They worshipped God and also practiced idolatry. The Jews rejected the Samaritans' offer to help rebuild the Temple because their survival depended on the preservation of their distinctive religion in its purity. The Samaritans thereupon became inveterate foes of the Jews, using every unscrupulous method to prevent them from building the Temple, constructing walls around Jerusalem, and establishing themselves in Judea.

or vulnerability to a nocturnal attack. He inspired the people to rebuild them and the gates, and apportioned the work among the men. The work was completed in fifty-two days, despite the sabotage of the Samaritans. Half the men stood guard while the other half worked.

The Samaritan leaders Sanballat, governor of Samaria, and Tuvia, his Ammonite aide, slandered the Jews to the Persian authorities to prevent construction; moreover, they tried to entrap Nehemiah.

Social Reforms

The Persian taxes were heavy and oppressive. The poor borrowed from the rich by mortgaging their houses and fields. When they could not pay their debts, the wealthy appropriated the poor people's property. Nehemiah rebuked the rich and forced them to remit the debts of the poor and return their property.

Security Measures for Jerusalem's Defense

Guards were stationed at the city gates.
   The gates were opened only during daylight hours.
   Loyal officials were given responsibility for defense.
   Settlements in Jerusalem were encouraged.

Religious Reform

After establishing national security, Nehemiah consolidated the nation by making the Torah the possession of all. It was a rallying point for the entire nation. He instituted certain practices that are observed to this day.

Reading the Torah in public:

The pulpit was placed in the midst of the synagogue.
The Torah was read every Saturday and holiday; there was
   a portion for each week.
Both men and women were obliged to hear it.
A sermon was given to expound the text so that it was
   understood by all and the religion did not become
   esoteric.

The observance of Succot was instituted. A covenant
was drawn up binding all the people to:

obey the Torah.
refrain from intermarriage.
not work on the Sabbath.
pay dues to support the Temple, priests, and Levites.

Nehemiah's Second Visit (in 432):

He found that the old evils had returned, and he eradi-
cated them by vigorous actions, such as:

Upholding the sanctity of the Temple and its precincts by
   literally throwing out Tuvia and his possessions. The
   Samaritan had been installed there by a corrupt High
   Priest.
Enforcing Sabbath observance by disallowing selling and
   commerce on that day.
Reinstituting support for Levites who served in the Temple.
Censure (again) of mixed marriages.

EZRA

Introduction

As indicated in the section on Nehemiah, there is a controversy about the precise time when Ezra lived. Tradition places him both before and contemporaneous with Nehemiah. Many modern scholars place Ezra *after* Nehemiah. The dating in this book follows the latter chronology.

A considerable portion of the book is in Aramaic: Chapters 4:8–6:18 and 7:12–26. Aramaic was used more than Hebrew as the vernacular language by Jews in the fourth century, by which time they were bilingual. The book also contains Akkadian and Persian words.

Several passages in this book are found in Nehemiah, with variations in genealogy and names.

Personal Background

Ezra had an outstanding personality and exercised a great influence on the development of Judaism. He was a strong leader and came at a critical time to save the Jewish religion and national life. He established the Torah as the center of Jewish life and was one of the founders of "the men of the Great Assembly." Ezra also preserved the identity of the Jewish people by his vigorous opposition to assimilation through intermarriage. He forced the termination of marriages with Gentile women who did not become Jews because of their negative influence on the next generation.

He came from a priestly family and was also a scribe. His name means "help."

Contents of the Book

The book is divided into two parts. Part 1, Chapters 1–6, reviews the history from Cyrus's Decree in 538 to the dedication of the Temple in 516.

1. Cyrus's decree:
    Allowed Jews to return to Judea.
    Permitted them to rebuild the Temple.
    Restored to the Jews the sacred Temple vessels that the Babylonians had looted.
2. Names of the clans, priests, and Levites who returned to Judea are listed.
3. The nation's religious life is described in terms of the building of the altar, the laying of the Temple's foundations, and the celebration of Succot.
4. The problem with the Samaritans is related: their offer of help, which was rejected, and their hampering of construction for twenty years.
5. Haggai and Zechariah's encouragement to continue rebuilding the Temple is followed by an inquiry by Persian officials. This leads to the report of Darius's decree authorizing the resumption of work.
6. The completion and dedication of the Temple is recorded, as is the celebration of Passover.

An interval of 119 years elapsed before the history was resumed in Part 2, in the year 397. The interval is blank except for the period of 445–432, which the Book of Nehemiah covers. Part 2, Chapters 7–10, records the arrival in Jerusalem of Ezra and his party and his subsequent activities.

7. In the seventh year of the reign of Artaxerxes II, 397, Ezra set out with his caravan, unarmed but with a

royal decree, to investigate conditions in Judea and with encouragement to teach the Torah. The king, Jews, and Gentiles all gave money for the Temple.

8.   A list of the people who accompanied Ezra is given. The list is similar to the list of those who accompanied Zerubabel. Apparently, when the book was redacted, it was no longer known who had come with Zerubabel and who with Ezra. However, a record of the settlers in Judea was kept.

9.   Ezra was aware of the prevalence of mixed marriages. Secular and religious leaders were the first to set a bad example. Ezra made a public confession to God of the people's sins.

10.   Ezra's public prayer catalyzed the people to repent. He concentrated his censure on intermarriage. Following the public prayer and confession, Ezra called a national assembly at which the men who refused to revoke their marriages were excommunicated and deprived of their property and other rights.

1, 2 CHRONICLES

Name and Place in the Canon

These are the last books in the Jewish canon. The Hebrew title can be freely translated as, "events of the times." The two books were originally one, and the division was made in the Septuagint. In the Christian canon, Chronicles follows Kings, which is historically logical. It is placed in the third division of the Hebrew Bible, because of the time of its canonization, which, of course, occurred after the Torah and Prophetic books. Talmudic tradition placed these books at the end of the Hebrew canon.

Date and Author

The author, whose name is not known, is sometimes called the "Chronicler." The books were probably written between 300 and 250 by a devout priest (*kohen*) or Levite who was also a historian and meticulous statistician. He compiled chronological lists of priestly families, Levitical families, and "fathers' houses" of the tribe of Judah, with special emphasis on the genealogy of David.

The Chronicler presented events from a religious viewpoint, seeing the universe as ruled by God. He believed that all occurrences were a result of divine reward for piety and good deeds and punishment for sin and apostasy.

The writer concentrated on the history of the Kingdom of Judah, with special attention to the reigns of David and Solomon, the Temple services, religious rituals and practices prescribed by the Torah, and the celebration of feasts, such as the observance of Passover by Hezekiah and Josiah. David, God's anointed and the chosen founder of a dynasty, is glorified, and no reference to his misconduct is made.

Historical Value of the Book

Since Chronicles was written with a religious and moral aim, it lacks the objectivity and balance of the other historical books. It contains many passages that have no parallel in Samuel and Kings, and others that give versions of events different from those found in the earlier books. The historical reliability of Chronicles in these cases is questioned by the authorities. Nonetheless, however, Chronicles contains valuable material that expands, supplements, and clarifies earlier works.

An example in which a narrative in Chronicles has no parallel in Kings is the description in the former of a fire coming down and consuming the burnt offering and sacrifice at the dedication of the Temple.

Divergences abound between the stories of David in 1 Chronicles and those related about him in 2 Samuel and 1 Kings. The latter books tell of David's wives and *concubines*, while Chronicles speaks only of his wives. Nor does the Chronicler mention David's seduction of Bathsheba and the illicit child born of that union. Solomon's accession to the throne in 1 Chronicles is treated in a summary and natural manner, with no reference to the intrigues that attended it, as described in 1 Kings.

In 2 Samuel, David's numbering of the people is said to have been instigated by God because of His anger at the Israelites. In the corresponding narrative, however, the Chronicler stated that Satan moved David to take the census. The nation suffered the loss of 70,000 lives as a result of David's sin.

The Chronicler was given to exaggeration at times, as exemplified by the price he stated that David paid for some land on which to build an altar to God. In 2 Samuel, he is said to have bought it from Arunah for *50 shekels of silver*, and in 1 Chronicles, David purchased it from Ornan (probably the same person with a different spelling of his name) for *600 shekels of gold*.

In general, the standard of this book in language and history is inferior to the other historical books.

Contents of the Books

The contents of the books fall into four sections.

1. *1 Chronicles 1–10: Chronology from Adam to Saul*

Genealogy of tribes of Israel and of priestly and Levitical families.
Specific genealogy of Saul and David.
Exile of Northern Kingdom to Assyria.
Names and places of priestly and Levitical cities.
Saul's death and burial.

2. *1 Chronicles 11–29: David's reign*

David's coronation.
Capture of Jebus (southeast part of Jerusalem, called the City of David).
Removal of the Ark and Tablets of the Law to the City of David.

Hiram's help to David in building his palace.

Victorious wars against Philistia, Moab, Aram, Edom, Ammon, and Amalek.

David's census, which led to divine punishment.[2]

Collection of materials for the future Temple.

List of the leaders of the military, civil, and religious organizations during the monarchy.

Appeal to the nation for offerings and blessings for Solomon.

3. 2 Chronicles 1–9: Solomon's Reign

Construction of the Temple with Hiram's help over a seven-year period.

Transfer of the Ark to the Holy of Holies amidst great national celebration.

Construction of Solomon's palace over a thirteen-year period.

Conscription of domestic labor and foreign captives for Solomon's building projects.

Building and strengthening of cities.

Queen of Sheba's visit and exchange of gifts.

Solomon's opulence, power, and death.

4. 2 Chronicles 10–36: Divided Kingdoms

Revolt of the northern tribes; establishment of Israel and Judah.

---

2. This story raises many perplexing theological and moral problems: (1) Why should taking a census be considered sinful? (2) If God instigated David to number the people, then David did not have free will. This contradicts the principle of free will. (3) Why should 70,000 people be punished for David's act, especially since he had been warned against it by Joab?

Review of the reigns of the kings of Israel until the fall of that kingdom, as recorded in 2 Kings.

Review of the reigns of the kings of Judah until its fall to Babylonia, the destruction of the Temple, and the exile of the Jews.

Israel existed from 932 to 722: 210 years, nineteen kings.

Judah lasted from 932 to 586: 346 years, twenty kings.

There was a continuous, uninterrupted Jewish kingdom for 444 years, from Saul's monarchy in 1030 to 586.

Famous Verses in Chronicles

1 Chronicles 29:10–13

David blessed the Lord before all the congregation and said: Blessed be You, O Lord, the God of Israel our father, forever and ever.

Yours, O Lord, is the greatness, and the power, and the glory, and the majesty; for all that is in the heaven and in the earth is Yours; Yours is the kingdom, O Lord, and You are exalted as head above all.

Both riches and honor come from You and You rule over all; and in Your hand is power and might; and in Your hand it is to make great and to give strength to all.

Now, our God, we thank You and praise Your glorious name.

[These verses of David's blessing, thanksgiving, and prayer are part of the morning service of the Jewish liturgy. The Christian Sunday liturgy includes similar verses.]

5

HOLY WRITINGS: WISDOM LITERATURE

Instruction in ancient Israel was provided by three classes of teachers:

Priests gave instruction in religious practices relating to worship, with divine authority.

Prophets communicated divine messages and visions, with divine authority.

Wise men counseled on proper behavior for the good life, harmonizing their teachings with the Torah and Prophets; they lacked divine authority.

Wisdom Literature in the Bible consists of Proverbs, Ecclesiastes, and Job. Some ideas found in this literature are expressed also in Psalms.

In the Apocrypha, Wisdom Literature is found in Ecclesiasticus, or the Wisdom of Ben Sira and the Wisdom of Solomon.

The Wisdom Literature was canonized by the end of the second century C.E.

121

The teachings in this literature, as in all the Jewish Bible, do not distinguish between the secular and religious. All human activity is within its scope. Wisdom was equated with morality, and wise men were equated with elders of the community.

Throughout Wisdom Literature is the concept that the highest wisdom is the fear of the Lord, which means reverence for God, not dread of Him.

PROVERBS

Meaning and Purpose of the Book

The Hebrew name for this book, *Mishlai*, has many meanings, such as "proverbs," "aphorisms," "maxims," "allegories," "parables," and "pithy sayings." The contents of the book include all these concepts.

The purpose of this volume is to give practical rules for living, especially to the young, without philosophical moralizing. It is concerned with the wisdom distilled from life's experiences by an older mentor. The book is the closest thing to a manual of ethics and behavior to serve as a pragmatic guide to help young people through life.

Authorship

The book probably had its beginnings in the reign of Solomon and material that the king and his wise men composed (tenth century B.C.E.) The book is attributed to Solomon, and some of his wise sayings have doubtless been retained therein. However, it is actually a distillation of wisdom from several ages and sages.

It was edited in the time of Hezekiah and includes material added over the next two centuries (eighth century B.C.E.).

Proverbs was issued in its final form by scribes living after Ezra. It was canonized in the second century C.E.

Contents of the Book

By way of introduction, the writer discourses on the nature and importance of wisdom. The motto of the book is stated: *The fear of the Lord is the beginning of knowledge.* (Fear should be understood as awe, not fright.)

The body of the book contains rules of practical, everyday ethics presented as aphorisms.

The book has thirty-one chapters. In the final chapter, the last twenty-two verses comprise a praise and tribute to the ideal wife.

Characteristics of the Book

1. Advice is given as if a teacher or mentor were speaking to a young disciple in order to guide him through life and a successful career and also show him how ethical behavior will benefit him.

2. Although the book uses the language of Judaism, it is directed to all people. The word *Israel* does not appear.

3. Wisdom and folly are represented as two women with contrasting ways of life. Wisdom is equated with morality. Folly is shown as leading to sin.

4. The book addresses people in every level and role in society: king, leaders, judges, tradesmen, farmers, and the poor.

5. It offers shrewd advice in every relationship:

Treatment of friends and the poor
Fidelity between spouses
Rearing of children
Behavior toward neighbors
Dangers of signing a surety for others
Perils of overconfidence in oneself
Warnings against seduction by foreign, faithless women

6. The book shows remarkable candor in its observations, for example: wealth has its advantages and poverty, its drawbacks; and be cautious in the presence of the powerful.

7. Verses 10–31 in the last chapter are a paean to the ideal wife, stating that her charity, industriousness, and selflessness are a blessing to her family and bring honor to her husband. The poem is traditionally recited on Sabbath eve by a husband to his wife or by sons to their widowed mother. It is in the form of an alphabetical acrostic.

Famous Verses in Proverbs

There are hundreds of worthy phrases and maxims in Proverbs. The following verses include only a smattering of the innumerable subjects and insightful sayings in this book.

1:7   The fear of the Lord is the beginning of wisdom. [This verse appears with slightly different words and word order in Proverbs 9:10 and 15:33 and also in Psalm 111:10, Job 28:28, and Ecclesiasticus 1:14.]

1:8   Hear, my son, the instruction of your father
And forsake not the teaching of your mother.
[This is also found in 6:20.]

3:12   For whom the Lord loves, He corrects
Even as a father, the son in whom he delights.

3:17   Her ways are ways of pleasantness
And all her paths are peace.

3:18   She is a tree of life to those that lay hold of her
And happy is everyone who holds her fast.

[These verses are included in the Jewish liturgy when the Torah is returned to the Ark in the synagogue.]

6:6   Go to the ant, you sluggard
        Consider her ways and be wise.

7:22   He goes after her [a harlot] suddenly
        As an ox that goes to the slaughter.

10:1   A wise son makes a father glad;
        And a foolish son is the grief of his mother.

10:12   Hatred stirs up strife;
        But love covers all transgressions.

11:12   He who shows contempt to his neighbor lacks
        understanding
        But a man of discernment holds his peace.

11:16   A gracious woman obtains honor;
        And tyrannical men obtain wealth.

11:22   As a ring of gold in a swine's snout
        Is the lack of discretion in a beautiful woman.

13:12   Hope deferred makes the heart sick;
        But desire fulfilled is a tree of life.

14:1   Every wise woman builds her house;
        And the foolish one tears it down with her own
        hands.

14:20   The poor is hated even by his own neighbor;
        But the rich have many friends.
        [Similar to 19:4.]

15:1   A soft answer turns away wrath;
        But a grievous word arouses anger.

16:18   Pride goes before destruction
        And a haughty spirit before a fall.

16:32   He who is slow to anger is superior to the mighty;
        And he who rules his spirit [is superior to] the con-
        queror of a city.

17:1   Better is a dry morsel and tranquillity within
        Than a house full of feasting with strife.

17:28 Even a fool, when he is silent is considered wise.

18:22 Whoever finds a wife finds a great good.

22:1 A good name is preferable to great riches.
[Similar to Ecclesiastes 7:1.]

22:6 Educate a child in the way he should go
And even when he is old, he will not depart
from it.

22:7 The rich rule over the poor,
And a borrower is a servant to the lender.

22:10 Expel the scorner and contention will leave.

23:22 Hearken to your father who begot you,
And despise not your mother when she is old.

27:1 Boast not of tomorrow,
Because you don't know what the day may bring.

27:10 Better a near neighbor than a far-off brother.

30:21 Under three things the earth quakes,
And under four it cannot endure:

30:22 Under a slave who becomes king
And a scoundrel when he is well off;

30:23 Under an unloved wife when she is reestablished
And a maid who becomes mistress of the house.

31:30 Grace is deceitful and beauty is vain
But a woman who fears the Lord should be
praised.

ECCLESIASTES

Meaning

Ecclesiastes, a Greek word, is called *Kohelet* in Hebrew. The word in Hebrew and Greek refers to one who convenes a congregation or assembly and is sometimes personified to mean a preacher. The purpose of the author is a search for life's meaning. Ecclesiastes is read in the synagogue on the holiday of Succot (Tabernacles).

Authorship

The putative author is King Solomon, which gave prestige to the book and the impetus to include it in the canon. According to legend, Solomon wrote this book in the bitterness of old age.

Kohelet had resources of great wealth, luxury, power, and wisdom—all of which characterized Solomon. *Kohelet* also engaged in follies, as did Solomon, bringing unsettled conditions to his land and the eventual breakup of the kingdom.

Most scholars place the book in the third century B.C.E. and attribute it to an unknown author.

Purpose and Characteristics

The book is a search for truth and the meaning of life. The writing is pessimistic, skeptical, and contradictory. Ecclesiastes is paradoxical and juxtaposes faith and futility, piety and scepticism. The overriding theme is, "Vanity of vanities, all is vanity" (1:2). Stated otherwise, all efforts and achievements are futile and everything passes.

Contents of the Book

1. It is vain and to no avail to:

Pursue knowledge and wisdom
Achieve wealth
Seek worldly pleasures
Attain honor because everything is transient and of only
   temporary satisfaction.

2. However, *Kohelet* contradicted himself by saying:

Wisdom can save a person's life and can get him through
   life better than if he lacks it. Wisdom has merits over
   strength.
Man should enjoy all the prosperity and pleasures life
   affords him.
A good reputation is the most important aim in life.

3. *Kohelet* said that it is futile to do the following:

a. To work hard and be ambitious, because the fruits of
   one's efforts may pass on to unworthy heirs and because the lazy person gets his necessities also, and
   without struggle.
b. To pursue justice because men pervert justice and
   because the end of everyone is death, whether he was
   good or evil.
c. To achieve royal popularity because a poor wise youth
   may replace a king on his throne (as David replaced
   Saul).
d. To be miserly and acquisitive because people leave the
   world as they entered it: empty-handed. Moreover,
   misers are never satisfied and always need to increase
   their possessions. They do not even enjoy what they
   have.

4. Cynical observations of *Kohelet*:

a. Government is corrupt; officials oppress the poor; bribery is rampant.
b. The righteous suffer and the evil prosper (noted also in Habakkuk, Jeremiah, Job, and Psalm 73).
c. Everything is ordained by a fixed scheme of God; man's efforts and prayers will not change events; a person cannot know whether his behavior will bring him happiness or grief.
d. No matter how hard a man may try to understand God's government of the universe, he will not learn it.

5. Pessimistic observations and their contradictions

a. It is better not to be born than to be born.
b. It is better to be stillborn than to have a long life without satisfaction.

However, conversely, *Kohelet* also said that life is to be preferred to death.

c. Providence is inscrutable; the good and wicked can reap the same reward from God.

Nonetheless, the writer also warned of God's eventual judgment of man's behavior.

6. Advice

a. Enjoy life as much as possible.
b. Working for something gives more pleasure than accumulating possessions.
c. Practice moderation: do not be overly wise or righteous nor overly wicked or foolish.

d. Do not pay attention to everything said about you.

e. Be expedient and circumspect in the presence of autocrats, rather than forthright and courageous.

f. Do not waste time concentrating on what catastrophes can happen; take action despite life's uncertainties and one's lack of control over circumstances.

g. Rejoice while you still have youth and vigor, because both are fleeting.

7. Epilogue: opinion is divided on the authenticity of the last two verses of the book. Some consider it an editorial addition by a scribe, for the tone changes, to one of piety and faith. There is an admonition to fear God and keep His commandments and an assurance that God will judge everything.

Famous Verses in Ecclesiastes

As in Proverbs, there are numerous pithy and note-worthy verses in this book, which reveal great psychological insight. The following verses are but a handful culled from the work.

1:2 Vanity of vanities, all is vanity.
[This verse is found throughout the book and reflects its basic theme.]

1:5 The sun also rises and goes down
And hastens to the place where it arose.

1:7 All the rivers run into the sea
Yet the sea is not full.

1:9 That which has been is that which shall be,
And what has been done is what shall be done;
And there is nothing new under the sun.

1:18 For in much wisdom is much vexation;
And he who increases knowledge increases pain.

2:13   I saw that wisdom is superior to folly
        As light is superior to darkness.
3:1   To everything there is a season,
        And a time and a purpose under heaven:
3:2   A time to be born and a time to die,
        A time to plant and a time to pluck up what is
        planted;
3:3   A time to kill and a time to heal,
        A time to break down and a time to build up;
3:4   A time to weep and a time to laugh,
        A time to mourn and a time to dance;
3:5   A time to cast away stones and a time to gather
        them,
        A time to embrace and a time to refrain from em-
        bracing;
3:6   A time to seek and a time to lose,
        A time to keep and a time to cast away;
3:7   A time to tear and a time to sew,
        A time to keep silent and a time to speak;
3:8   A time to love and a time to hate,
        A time for war and a time for peace.
4:6   Better is a handful of quietness
        Than both hands full of labor and striving after
        wind.

4:13   Better is a poor and wise child than an old and
        foolish king.
7:1   A good name is better than precious oil.
        [Similar to Proverbs 22:1.]
7:11   Wisdom is good with an inheritance.

7:12   For wisdom is a defense as money is a defense;
        But the superiority of knowledge is that wisdom
        can preserve the life of one who has it.
7:16   Do not be overrighteous or oversmart;
        Why should you destroy yourself?

9:4   Where there is life there is hope;
For a living dog is better than a dead lion.

9:11   I saw again that the race is not to the swift, nor
battle to the strong;
Neither bread to the wise, nor wealth to the smart,
nor favor to the skilled;
But time and chance happen to them all.

11:1   Cast your bread upon the waters
For you will find it in many days.

12:7   And the dust will return to the earth as it was
And the spirit returns to God who gave it.

JOB

Introduction

Job has been recognized throughout the ages and world as one of the greatest books of all time. It is a superb poem, in dialogue form, with narrative prologue and epilogue in prose.

The author and date of the book are unknown. There is much speculation, since there are no allusions to historical events or persons, although the name Job appears in Ezekiel. Some scholars speculate that it was written between 600 and 400 B.C.E. and underwent many revisions until the year 200 B.C.E. There is debate as to whether Job existed or was a parable and a product of the author's imagination. There is even speculation among some scholars as to whether Job was a Hebrew or Edomite. This latter idea derives mainly from the mention of Teman as the geographical background of Job's friends. There is evidence in the story of strong Jewish content, whether the character was real or imaginary.

Contents of the Book

Prose Prologue

The book opens with scenes that alternate between the land of Uz, where Job lived, and Heaven, where there was a meeting of God's celestial court (which included the Satan).[1]

---

1. Satan is perceived as a heavenly adversary, which is the meaning of his name. He is referred to as *the* satan, or "adversary." Other meanings of the word are "accuser" or "prosecutor."

Job was an exemplary man of virtue and piety who enjoyed great wealth and an ideal family, consisting of seven sons and three daughters. Then Satan cast suspicion on Job's unselfish motives for his righteousness. God thereupon gave Job into Satan's hands to test his fidelity to Him.

Despite the loss of his wealth, children, and health, Job did not blaspheme the Lord.

Three friends, Eliphaz, Bildad, and Zophar, came to comfort Job. They sat in silence for a week, appalled at Job's suffering and misery.

Poetic Dialogues between Job and His Three Friends

There are three cycles of discourses. In each one Job speaks first and is followed by his friends. The drama consists of the speakers' thoughts and emotions.

The friends expressed the prevailing belief that the righteous and wicked receive their just deserts on earth. Suffering is Divine punishment for sinfulness, and prosperity is the reward for righteousness.

Job, who must have held this belief at one time, protested his innocence and piety. The friends urged Job to accept his suffering as punishment and correction for his wrongdoing and to ask God's forgiveness. God may then relent. They offered no comfort to Job. Instead, they escalated their arguments, reproaching him and making cruel accusations against him. They insisted that God was just in His ways with man.

Job maintained his integrity, refusing to concede that he deserved his fate. In his agony, he accused God of injustice and arbitrary rule, saying that He destroyed the innocent with the wicked.

Job repeatedly entreated and challenged God to appear in a tribunal to explain why He had afflicted him and to state the charges against him. Job insisted that he wanted to establish his innocence and to affirm his moral goodness. Job eventually reached the belief that God would vindicate him. He had no hope of such help from his friends.

Intrusion and Argument of Elihu

Elihu, a garrulous youth, rebuked both Job and the three friends; the former for justifying himself instead of God, and the latter for condemning Job without refuting his arguments.

His contribution to the mystery of suffering was that it is a warning and a moral discipline to the afflicted.

Elihu disappeared as suddenly as he appeared; he is not heard from or referred to again.

The Answers of the Lord from Out of the Whirlwind

God displayed the wonders of creation and the universe to Job. He posed a series of questions that exposed Job's (and, therefore, mankind's) ignorance of the mysteries of God's governance of the universe. *Nor did God explain those mysteries to Job.* Job was humbled (perhaps intimidated), and he repented of his presumptuousness in criticizing God's rule.

Prose Epilogue

Job was vindicated by God. His friends were condemned for not speaking the truth about suffering, as did "God's servant, Job." Job's trial was over; God brought back his children to him and restored his prosperity and happiness (42:10–17).

Meaning of the Book

Job is a challenge to, and refutation of, the doctrine found in many other Bible books that a person's suffering is a sign of his sinfulness, while prosperity is proof of his piety. The book also affirms that the just are often afflicted, while the wicked are frequently successful. All this corroborates mankind's experience and observations.

As for the tormenting question of *why* a just God allows this to happen, the book does not provide a clear or explicit answer. The explanation given is that human beings, because of their finite intelligence, cannot fathom the infinite wisdom of God or comprehend the mystery of His rule. However, the spiritual integrity of righteous people will enable them to be at peace with God and to endure their suffering. Moreover, they will never feel cut off from God, no matter how afflicted.

Famous Verses in Job

1:21   Naked came I out of my mother's womb
And naked shall I return thither;
The Lord gave and the Lord has taken away;
Blessed be the name of the Lord.

2:10   Shall we receive good from God and the evil not receive?

7:10   Why do You not pardon my transgression
And take away my iniquity?
For now I shall lie down in the dust;
And You will seek me, but I shall not be.

12:2   Of course you are everybody

And when you die all wisdom will perish with
you.
[Job was being sarcastic here.]

12:3   I have understanding as well as you
I am not inferior to you;
Who doesn't know things like these?
[Similar to 13:2.]

12:12   In aged men there is wisdom
And with length of days there is understanding

13:15   Let Him slay me, I have nothing to hope for
I only wish to justify my conduct to His face.

13:16   This shall also be my salvation,
That a hypocrite cannot come before Him.

14:1   Man that is born of woman
Is of few days and full of trouble.

14:2   He comes forth like a flower and withers
He flees as a shadow which does not remain.

19:20   My bone cleaves to my skin and to my flesh.
And I have escaped by the skin of my teeth.

19:21   Have pity on me, have pity on me, my friends;
For the hand of God has touched [afflicted] me.

19:25   As for me, I know that my Redeemer lives
And that at the end He will appear on earth.

19:26   Even after my skin has been torn from my flesh
Still will I hope that I will see God.

26:2   How you have helped me who is without power!
How you have saved the arm that has no strength!

26:3   How you have counseled one who has no wis-
dom,
And gave plenty of sound knowledge!
[Job's sarcasm is palpable here.]

28:28   The fear of the Lord is wisdom
And to depart from evil is understanding.
[Similar to Psalm 110:10 and Proverbs 9:10.]

34:3   For the ear tests words
       As the palate tastes food.

38:1   Then the Lord answered Job out of the whirlwind.

42:5   I had heard of You by the hearing of the ear;
       But now my eyes see You;

42:6   Therefore I abhor my words and repent
       Seeing I am dust and ashes.

In several verses Job denies reincarnation, namely:

7:9   As the cloud is consumed and vanishes,
       So he who goes down to the grave shall come up
       no more.

14:12   So man lies down and rises not;
       Till the heavens are no more they shall not wake
       Nor be roused out of their sleep.

14:14   If a man dies, shall he live again?
       All the days of my service I would wait
       Till my change [release] would come.

6

THE REST OF
THE HOLY WRITINGS

The remaining books in the Hagiographa do not easily fit into the divisions (historical books or wisdom literature) into which the other books fall that are in this section of the Hebrew Bible. Each of the four books has its own genre.

Song of Songs is a series of love poems. Ruth is the tale of a devoted Moabite girl to her Jewish mother-in-law. Lamentations bewails the fall of Jerusalem and the suffering of its population. The Book of Psalms consists of collections of poems often set to music and used in the liturgy, first of the Temple and then of the synagogue.

The first three books are related to specific historical periods in the history of Israel. Ruth occurs in the time of the Judges, Song of Songs occurs during King Solomon's reign, and Lamentations was written by Jeremiah at the fall of Judah. Since the Book of Psalms was composed over many centuries, they do not fit into any specific historical period but rather belong to many eras in Jewish history.

Inasmuch as these four books do not fall into any of the categories into which I have organized my work, I have chosen to discuss them in a separate chapter. It must be apparent to all readers that none of these books is of less value and beauty than the preceding nine.

SONG OF SONGS

Introduction

According to tradition, Solomon wrote Song of Songs in his youth, Proverbs in his middle years, and Ecclesiastes in his old age.

Scholars differ as to the author and date of Song of Songs, but there is strong evidence, in both style and content, that it was composed in Solomon's time in northern Israel and associated with the king.

The title, Song of Songs, means the choicest of songs. It is a series of lyric love songs within a story.

The book is read at Passover. The name of God appears only as a suffix to a word, *shalhevet-yah* ("flame of the Lord," 8:6). Although specific mention of God's name and the religion of Israel are absent from this book, it is a favorite among Jews.

Narrative

The book is a love story about a beautiful peasant girl from Shunem or Shulem in the Jezreel Valley, who was a shepherdess to her family's flocks. She is anonymous except for the reference to her in one verse as the Shulamite [girl], which recalls the name of her village. She loved a shepherd of her village, but her brothers disapproved of the union. They transferred her work from the pasture to the vineyard, hoping to prevent her from meeting her lover.

One day, while tending the vines, she was seen by King Solomon's servants as they passed the village on their way to his summer residence in northern Israel.

They were impressed with her beauty and tried to persuade her to accompany them. She refused and was taken captive to the king's chambers.

As soon as the king saw her, he fell madly in love with her. He praised her beauty and tried to convince her to abandon her shepherd for the love and wealth he could give her. The ladies of the court joined in trying to dissuade the girl from her humble swain. However, she was adamant in her fidelity.

During her stay in the palace, she yearned for her lover and was taunted by the court ladies that he had abandoned her. She became so agitated that she spoke to him as if he were with her and dreamed that he had come to rescue her and return her to her home. Awakened from her dream, she rushed out to the streets at night and was roughly treated by the watchmen, who misjudged her character.

The king finally realized the constancy of the sheperdess's love for her shepherd and reluctantly allowed her to return to her home and lover. The latter joined her, and they returned to Shunem to a warm welcome.

The story ends on a high note, celebrating the triumph of true love over all temptations and hardships.

Interpretation and Moral of the Book

Some modern commentators consider the book a collection of nuptial love songs sung at wedding feasts. The content and language are noble and lofty, with none of the abandonment of pagan marriage feasts.

Jewish scholars from Akiba (second century C.E.) to Rashi and Maimonides (eleventh and twelfth centuries,

respectively) saw in the story an allegory of the relationship between God and Israel. Otherwise, they would
not have had reason to accept into the canon a secular
love tale or series of rustic wedding songs.

The allegory seen in the story is the loyalty that Jews
have displayed toward their faith throughout the ages,
which is reflected in the fidelity of the Shulamite girl to
her lover. Like the Shulamite, Jews were forcibly taken
from their homeland. Many suitors clamored for acceptance—Rome, the Church, Islam—demanding that Jews
exchange their God for another. However, also like the
Shulamite, the Jews' love for their ancient faith could
not be extinguished by temptations of wealth and ease,
and like the Shulamite, they suffered for their refusal to
be unfaithful. The mocking question of the court ladies,
"Where has your beloved gone?" (6:1) has its parallel in
the taunt of the nations to the Jews, "Where is your God
to help you?"

In the end, love and fidelity emerge triumphant. Love
of a mate or a faith strengthens and hallows its possessors.

Famous Verses in Song of Songs

1:5   I am black and comely,
1:15   Behold, you are fair, my love; behold you are fair,
       Your eyes are like doves.
2:1   I am a rose of Sharon
       A lily of the valleys.

2:11   For lo the winter is past,
       The rain is over and gone;
2:12   The flowers appear on the earth;
       The time of singing has come,
       And the voice of the turtle [dove] is heard in our land.

2:13   The fig tree puts forth her green figs
And the vines in blossom give forth their fragrance.
Arise my love, my fair one, and come away.
[This is a description of springtime in Israel and in many other places.]

5:8   I adjure you, O daughters of Jerusalem,
If you find my beloved, what will you tell him?
That I am love-sick.
[This book is perhaps the first to label and diagnose "love-sickness," which is also mentioned in 2:5.]

6:3   I am my beloved's and my beloved is mine.

8:6   For love is strong as death,
Jealousy is cruel as the grave.

8:7   Many waters cannot quench love
Neither can the floods drown it;
If a man would give all the substance of his house for love,
He would be utterly despised.

RUTH

Introduction

The author and date of composition are disputed. According to Jewish tradition, Samuel wrote this book. Others believe that it was composed during the Monarchy (after 1030 B.C.E.); still others date it in the postexilic period of Nehemiah or Ezra (465–380 B.C.E.). Some scholars date the book in the first century B.C.E.

The book is a beautiful epic, in four chapters, of love and devotion in a pastoral setting at the time of the Judges (around the twelfth century B.C.E.) Both the style and plot are simple and direct.

It is read in the synagogue during Shavuot, the holiday that commemorates the giving of the Law at Sinai and celebrates the spring harvest. The story takes place in Bethlehem during the harvest. Just as Israel accepted the Law of Moses at Sinai, so did Ruth accept the faith of Israel.

Ruth is the Hebrew name most often taken by female converts to Judaism. Part of Ruth's entreaty to her mother-in-law, Naomi, is included in the conversion ceremony of Reform Judaism: "Your people shall be my people and your God, my God."

Narrative

In Bethlehem of Judah lived Elimelech, a prosperous man; his wife, Naomi; and their two sons, Mahlon and Chilion. The family left Judea because of a famine and went to reside in Moab. Elimelech died shortly after settling there. His sons married Moabite women, Orpah and Ruth, and died childless. Ten years after settling in

Moab, Naomi decided to return to Judah, where the famine had ceased. She was now widowed, bereft of her children, homeless, and destitute. Her daughters-in-law set out with her. Orpah was persuaded to return to her home, but Ruth clung to Naomi. The two women arrived in Bethlehem in the early spring at the time of the barley harvest.

Ruth, who was kind, considerate, and hard-working, went into the fields to glean in order to maintain herself and Naomi. She gleaned in the fields of Boaz, a relative of her deceased father-in-law. Boaz was attracted to this modest, devoted young woman and showed more than a paternal interest in her.

When Naomi realized Boaz's interest in Ruth, she told her to go to the threshing floor, where Boaz retired for the night after work. Ruth followed Naomi's advice and gently reminded Boaz that, as a kinsman, he owed certain duties to Naomi and herself.

There was a closer relative than Boaz who had priority in redeeming Elimelech's family and, therefore, in marrying Ruth. The following morning, Boaz lost no time in going to the city gate, where the elders gathered to deal with claims and litigations. He assembled ten men along with the kinsman, and offered the latter the option of buying Elimelech's land and marrying Ruth, with whom he would (have to) raise an heir. The relative declined, and thus, the duty fell to Boaz.

Boaz thereupon married Ruth. She bore a son, Oved, who in turn begot Jesse, who fathered David.

Purpose and Value of the Book

1. It shows a beautiful picture of peace and tranquillity in Israel during the period of the Judges. Thus, we are

not left solely with the impression of violence and war during that period, as is recorded in the Book of Judges.

2. It conveys a strong message in favor of conversion, when done in good faith. A convert had the distinction of being the ancestress of the most famous king in Israel.

3. The book serves as an admonition against leaving Israel, even in times of famine and hardship. The death of the father and two sons was interpreted as their punishment for leaving their homeland.

4. The book shows the customs and religious observance of the simple people during the period of the Judges, as well as a love for their land.

5. The book provides the genealogy of David.

Famous Verses in Ruth

1:16 And Ruth said: "Entreat me not to leave you and to return from following after you; for where you go, I will go; and where you lodge, I will lodge; your people shall be my people, and your God, my God.

1:17 Where you die, I will die and there will I be buried; the Lord do so to me and more also if aught but death part you and me."

2:12 The Lord recompense your work and may your reward be complete from the Lord, the God of Israel, under whose wings you came to take refuge.

LAMENTATIONS

Introduction

Lamentations is known by two names in Hebrew. The first, *Echah*, comes from the initial word in the book, as is the practice with the names of the books of the Pentateuch. The Talmud gave a second title to the book based on its contents, which is *Kinot*, meaning "elegies" or "lamentations." The book is read in synagogues on the Fast of the Ninth of Av, when the destruction of both Temples is commemorated: 586 B.C.E. and 70 C.E.

Jeremiah is credited with writing Lamentations. This ascription is generally accepted. (However, as with all Biblical matters, there are some scholars who disagree.) The prophet was fated to foretell the destruction of Jerusalem and the fall of Judea. The fulfillment of his prophecies filled this compassionate man with grief. His own tragic life was a reflection of the greater tragedy which befell his people.

Contents of the Book

The book comprises five chapters, each of which is a separate elegy. Each poem is an emotional, heartrending outpouring of the prophet's soul.

The overall theme is a lament for Judea and Jerusalem, which had been destroyed by the Babylonians in 586 B.C.E. The suffering of the inhabitants during and after the siege is described in harrowing detail: the starvation, thirst, disease, imprisonment, degradation, and death are vividly portrayed and the desolation and ruin of Judea are recorded.

Jeremiah confessed the sins of the people and their leaders, who misled them into allying themselves with Egypt and opposing Babylonia. He insisted on resignation to God's will and he interpreted the exile and suffering as punishment for the nation's sins.

The poems invoked God's vengeance on Edom for its treachery and malice in cutting off the escape of Judean refugees and gloating over Judea's fall. This was the theme of Obadiah's prophecy.

The last poem is more a prayer than a lament. It is an account of Judea's tragic condition laid before God in the hope of securing His compassion for the remnant of Israel. Jeremiah prayed for the restoration of God's favor, which would bring the return of the Judeans to their land.

Structure of the Book

Four of the five poems are alphabetic in structure. Chapters 1, 2, and 4 each have twenty-two verses beginning with successive letters of the Hebrew alphabet (which contains twenty-two letters). Chapter 3 has sixty-six verses following a triple alphabet. Chapter 5 has twenty-two verses, but not in alphabetical order.

Famous Verses in Lamentations

1:1   How does the city sit solitary
That was full of people!
How has she become a widow!
She that was great among the nations,
And princess among the provinces
How has she become a tributary!

3:44   You have covered Yourself with a cloud,
        So that no prayer can pass through.

4:5   Those who fed on dainties
        Are desolate in the streets;
        They who were brought up in scarlet
        Lie prostrate on dunghills.

4:9   Those who are slain with the sword are better off
        Than those who are stricken with hunger.

5:21   Turn us O Lord unto You and we shall be returned;
        Renew our days as of old.
        [This is part of a Sabbath prayer.]

PSALMS

Meaning and Description

The word for psalms in Hebrew, *tehilim*, means praises.

Psalms are Hebrew lyric poetry probably inaugurated by King David and imitated by later generations.

They are hymns of praise that were sung by Levite choirs in the Temple to instrumental accompaniment.

Today, Psalms are an important part of the synagogue liturgy on Sabbath and holidays.

There are 150 psalms distributed in five books: 1–41, 42–72, 73–89, 90–106, and 107–150.

This is the longest book in the Bible.

Authorship

The psalms were traditionally attributed to David. Seventy-three have a superscription to David, which may mean either "by David," "concerning David," or "in David's style." However, they were not all written by David. Many of these and other psalms refer to historical events occurring long after his reign.

Twelve psalms are attributed to Asaph, a Levite musician who arranged music in the Temple and was appointed by David.

There are other superscriptions, and many psalms have none at all.

There are several collections in the Book of Psalms:

Songs of Ascents (Psalms 120–134)
Korahite Psalms (Psalms 42–49, 84, 87, 88)
Hallel Psalms (Psalms 111–118, of praise to God)

Song writing was an ancient art in Israel before Psalms, as in the Song at the Red Sea (Exodus 15) and the Song of Deborah (Judges 5).

Subject Matter of the Psalms

Praise of God, Torah, Zion, David and his dynasty.
Elegies: suffering of the nation and individuals for sin in accordance with the accepted belief that sin leads to punishment.
Ethics: instruction in the right way of living:
    Reflections on hardships and struggles
    Doubts in the face of the triumph of the wicked.

Religious and Ethical Doctrines in the Psalms

GOD

Man's awareness of His power.
His interest in His people and in all nations.
His power and righteousness.

MAN

His duty to praise God in words and deeds.

SIN

Defined as rebellion against God through paganism or immoral acts against people.

PROBLEM OF THE TRIUMPH OF EVIL

Concern with, and protest against, the success of the wicked and the suffering of the righteous.
Faith in eventual retribution and justice.

EXILE

Pleas to restore Zion and end the captivity.

Rejoicing at the return to Zion.

Imprecations against Edom, Babylonia, Aram, and other traditional enemies and persecutors of Israel.

ISRAEL AND ZION

God chose Zion as the center on earth for His abode. Israel is to spread the Law from Zion to the world. Messianic hope was that all mankind would acknowledge God as the supreme Judge and King and accept His Torah as law.

Characteristics of Hebrew Poetry

Rhyme is rare; meter is unknown; but there is a rhythmical beat.

Chanted in antiphonal form, which gave rise to parallelism, the most noted feature of Hebrew poetry:

SYNONYMOUS (PS. 15:1)

Lord, who shall sojourn in Your tabernacle

Who shall dwell upon Your holy mountain?

ANTITHETIC (PS. 1:6)

For the Lord regards the way of the righteous

But the way of the wicked shall perish.

SYNTHETIC (PS. 1:1)

Happy is the man who has not walked in the counsel of the wicked,

Nor stood in the way of sinners,

Nor sat in the seat of the scornful.

Distinctive Psalms

Psalms 1 and 2 are the introduction to the book.

Psalm 15 expresses the Hebrew ideal of human behavior.

Psalm 23 is the most popular psalm: "The Lord is my shepherd."

Psalm 29 is a poetic picture of a storm ending with peace; it is sung in the Sabbath liturgy.

Psalms 79 and 137 are about the Babylonian destruction of Jerusalem and the Temple. They are recited on the Ninth of Av.

Psalms 92, 95, and 96 are recited at the Friday-night liturgy.

Psalms 113 and 114: almost every verse is famous and taken from another part of the Bible.

Psalm 117 is the shortest psalm, with two beautiful verses.

Psalm 119 is the longest psalm and chapter in the Bible, with 175 verses.

Psalm 126 is the blessing at the end of the meal.

Psalm 145 is read responsively in the daily and Sabbath prayers in synagogue.

Famous Verses in Psalms

8:5   What is man that You are mindful of him?
       And the son of man that You think of him?
8:6   Yet You have made him but little lower than
       the angels
       And have crowned him with glory and honor.
       [From the liturgy on Yom Kippur or the Day of
       Atonement, similar to Ps. 144:3.]

16:8	I have set the Lord always before me; Surely He is at my right hand. I shall not be moved.
24:1	The earth is the Lord's and the fullness thereof; The world and those who dwell in it. [Similar to Ps. 89:12.]
34:4	Magnify the Lord with me; And let us exalt His name together.
34:9	Happy is the man that takes refuge in Him.
34:14	Keep your tongue from evil, And your lips from speaking guile. [The three preceeding verses are in the Sabbath liturgy.]
37:25	I have been young and now am old Yet I have not seen the righteous forsaken Nor his seed begging bread. [Part of the Blessing after the Meal.]
71:9	Cast me not out in my old age When my strength fails, forsake me not. [In the Yom Kippur liturgy.]
79:6	Pour out your wrath upon the nations that have not known You And upon the Kingdoms that call not upon Your name.
79:7	For they have devoured Jacob And laid waste his habitation. [Also in Jeremiah and the Passover Haggadah.]
79:10	Why should the Gentiles say, "Where is their God?" [Also in Exodus 32:12, Numbers 14:13, and Ps. 115:2.]
84:5	Happy are they who dwell in Your house They are ever praising You. Selah.
84:13	Lord of hosts, Happy is the man who trusts in You.

[The above two verses are in the Sabbath liturgy.]

90:4   For a thousand years in Your sight
          Are but as yesterday when it is past
          And as a watch in the night.

96:11   Let the heavens be glad and the earth rejoice
          Let the sea roar and all that live in it.

106:1   Give thanks to the Lord for He is good;
          For His mercy endures forever.
          [Also found in the first verses of Ps. 107, 118, and 138.]

115:4   Their idols are silver and gold;
          The work of men's hands.

115:5   They have mouths, but they speak not;
          They have eyes, but they see not.

115:6   They have ears, but they hear not;
          They have noses, but they smell not.

115:7   They have hands, but they feel not;
          They have feet, but they walk not;
          Neither can they make a sound with their throat.

115:8   They who make them shall be like them;
          Yea, everyone who trusts in them.
          [Similar to Ps 135:15–18.]

115:16   The heavens are the heavens of the Lord
          But the earth He has given to mankind.

115:17   The dead do not praise the Lord
          Neither do those who go down into silence.

115:18   But we will bless the Lord
          From this time forth and forever. Halleluyah.

118:5   Out of the straits I called upon the Lord.

118:8   It is better to take refuge in the Lord
          Than to trust in man.

118:22   The stone which the builders rejected
          Has become the chief cornerstone.

119:105   Your word is a lamp unto my feet
          And a light unto my path.

119:157	Many are my persecutors and adversaries Yet I have not turned aside from Your testimonies.
121:1	I will lift my eyes to the mountains From whence will come my help?
121:2	My help comes from the Lord Who made heaven and earth.
121:4	Behold He Who guards Israel Shall neither slumber nor sleep.
121:8	The Lord shall guard your going out and coming in From this time forth and forever.
122:6	Pray for the peace of Jerusalem; May they who love you prosper.
128:5	The Lord will bless you out of Zion; And may you see the good of Jerusalem all the days of your life;
128:6	And may you see your children's children. Peace on Israel. [These two verses became a popular Israeli song.]
130:1	Out of the depths have I called you, O Lord.
137:1	By the rivers of Babylon There we sat down and wept When we remembered Zion.
137:2	Upon the willows in the midst We hung up our harps.
137:3	For there our captors asked of us words of song, And those who mocked us asked for mirth, "Sing us one of the songs of Zion."
137:4	How shall we sing the Lord's song In a foreign land?
137:5	If I forget you, O Jerusalem, Let my right hand forget her cunning.
137:6	Let my tongue cleave to the roof of my mouth If I remember you not;

If I set not Jerusalem
Above my highest joy.

149:6   Let the praises of God be in their mouth
And a two-edged sword in their hand.
[The Maccabean warriors had this verse in mind
when they went forth in battle against their
Syrian-Greek oppressors in 168 B.C.E.]

150:5   Praise Him with the loud cymbals
Praise Him with the clanging cymbals.

150:6   Let all who breathe praise the Lord
Halleluyah.
[These are the last verses in Psalms. They are
part of the Sabbath liturgy.]

GLOSSARY

Apocrypha Fourteen books that were not canonized by Jews and Protestants, but were by the Roman Catholic and Eastern Orthodox churches. The books were written between the second century B.C.E. and the first century C.E.

Aramaic Semitic language akin to Hebrew; the common language of the Middle East from the sixth century B.C.E. to the second century C.E.; the Bible contains Aramaic words.

B.C.E. Before the Common Era; secular term used instead of B.C.

C.E. Common Era; secular term used instead of A.D.

Covenant or *brit* A solemn agreement between God and the person with whom He chose to make the pact. The word in Hebrew is *brit*, which has the added meaning of circumcision because it is the outward sign of the Covenant.

Great Synagogue or **Great Assembly** (*haKnesset ha-Gedola* in Hebrew)   The supreme council during the Second Temple period. According to tradition, Haggai, Zechariah, and Malachi were its founders and Ezra was its leader during his mission in Jerusalem.

Havdalah   A home service at the conclusion of the Sabbath during which certain prayers and scriptural passages are read, a special candle is lit, and wine or milk is drunk. The word means *distinction*, and the ritual emphasizes the distinction between the sacredness of the Sabbath and the secular aspect of the rest of the week.

Israel   Another name for Jacob; also the name of the Northern Kingdom formed in the tenth century, which broke with Judah and Benjamin in the south (its capital was Samaria); now, the name of the modern Jewish state between the Mediterranean Sea and Jordan River. The area of Israel, including Judea and Samaria, is less than 8,000 sqare miles (about the size of New Jersey).

Judah   Eponymous name of one of the twelve tribes of Israel; name of the Southern Kingdom, with Jerusalem as its capital (sometimes called Judea).

Judean   A person from Judah or Judea; same as Jew (*yehudi* in Hebrew).

Judgment Day or the **Day of the Lord**   First articulated by the prophets. The term referred to God's judgment of the nations that oppressed Israel, as well as His judgment of Israel itself for the failure to live up to the ethical demands of the Torah. From about the second century B.C.E. to the second century C.E., the messianic idea developed in which the coming of a messiah or a messianic age was associated with Judgment Day.

Megiddo or **Har Megiddo** (Mount Megiddo) In the Jezreel Plain. This is the site of many historic battles. It is called *Armageddon* (a contraction of *Har Megiddo*) in the New Testament Book of Revelation and where it is said that the final battle between good and evil will take place.

Qumran Site of the caves on the northwest shore of the Dead Sea where the Dead Sea Scrolls were found. The people living in that area are believed to have been Essenes, a devout, reclusive Jewish sect. They disappeared after the Roman destruction of their settlement during the First Roman–Jewish War, 67–73 C.E.

Septuagint Greek translation of the Pentateuch in Alexandria, Egypt, by Jewish scholars; completed in 245 B.C.E. During the following two centuries the rest of the Bible was translated into Greek and included under the same title, although Jews did not necessarily translate it. The word means seventy in Latin and refers to the seventy (actually seventy-two) Jewish sages who had translated the Torah.

Talmud Consists of two parts: the Mishnah and the Gemara. The Mishnah is a codification of basic Jewish civil and religious law redacted between 200 and 225 C.E. The Gemara is an interpretation and elaboration of the Mishnah completed circa 500 C.E. It consists of opinions on civil, criminal, and religious law (*halachah*), as well as sermons, stories, folklore, anecdotes, and maxims (*haggadah*). There are two Talmuds: the Babylonian and the Jerusalem.

The Mishnah comprises six books. The Gemara is much longer and fills volumes. The former was written in Hebrew; the latter in Aramaic.

Tanakh   The Hebrew or Jewish Bible. It is actually an acronym formed from the Hebrew for *Torah* (Pentateuch), *Nevi'im* (Prophets), and *Ketuvim* (Hagiographa).

LOCATIONS OF ANCIENT COUNTRIES AND THEIR PRESENT NAMES

Aram   Ancient name for Syria; north and east of Israel.

Ammon   Ancient name for territory just east of the Jordan River in the present-day country of Jordan.

Assyria   Empire in the territory roughly of current-day northern Iraq; at its height of power during the eighth and seventh centuries B.C.E.; capital was Nineveh.

Babylonia   Empire in the territory roughly of central and southern Iraq today, in the lower valley of the southern Tigris and Euphrates Rivers; existed from about the year 2000 to the sixth century B.C.E.; known as Mesopotamia and/or Chaldea in its early history; capital was Babylon.

Edom (later called Idumea)   Southeast of the Dead Sea, between ancient Moab and Midian, in the present-day country of Jordan.

Egypt Country in North Africa on the Mediterranean and Red Seas whose history is intertwined with that of ancient Israel. Its borders in biblical times extended to Sudan and into present-day Ethiopia.

Media Kingdom northwest of ancient Persia, which is now part of Iran.

Midianites Occupied territory east of the Gulf of Akaba (which flows into the Red Sea); currently Saudi Arabia.

Moab East of Judah and south of the territory of Reuben, in the present-day country of Jordan.

Persia Ancient name for Iran, roughly the same territory; at its height of power from the sixth to fourth centuries B.C.E.

Philistia Comprised five cities: Ashkelon, Ashdod, Ekron, Gath, and Gaza, located along the southwestern coastal strip of Israel. The Philistines were a constant threat to the Israelites until they were subdued by David and his successors. The name *Palestine* comes from *Philistia*. The Romans first used that name in an effort to eradicate any connection of the Jews with the land of Israel. The Philistines as a people and culture had disappeared by the fifth century B.C.E.

Phoenicia Ancient name for Lebanon; its main cities were Sidon, Tyre, and Biblos.

BIBLIOGRAPHY

Aharoni, Yohanan, and Avi-Yonah, Michael. *The Modern Bible Atlas*. Rev. ed. London: George Allen and Unwin, 1982.

Bible Review (December 1992).

Biblical Archaeology Review (July–August 1985).

———. (May–June 1988).

Cohen, A., ed. *Soncino Books of the Bible*. London: Soncino Press, various years.

Encyclopedia Judaica. Jerusalem: Keter Publishing House, 1971.

Harper's Bible Dictionary. New York: Harper and Row, 1973.

Jewish Publication Society Torah Commentary. Philadelphia: Jewish Publication Society, 1991.

INDEX

ABOUT THE AUTHOR

Lillian C. Freudmann holds a master's degree in social work from Washington University in St. Louis. She has been a social worker in the United States and abroad. In Israel she was a caseworker with new immigrants and a probation officer with juvenile delinquents. Mrs. Freudmann has taught courses in Hebrew and Bible and has lectured on the Bible and Jewish subjects. She currently teaches Bible courses in an adult program associated with the University of Connecticut School of Continuing Education. Her first book, *Antisemitism in the New Testament*, was published in 1994 and was critically acclaimed. She has five children and two grandchildren.